79
NETWORK
MARKETING
TIPS

"I will do today what others won't do, so I can do tomorrow what others can't do."

"If you want to change some things in your life, you've got to change some things in your life."

"Life is not about how many breaths you take, but about how many moments take your breath away."

79 NETWORK MARKETING TIPS

FOR FAST-TRACK SUCCESS

Discover the need-to-know insider advice to catapult you to the top

WES LINDEN

NOAH'S HOUSE PUBLISHING

Published by Noah's House Publishing
www.noahshousepublishing.com

www.weslinden.com/79tips

Contents

Acknowledgements   **vi**

Foreword by Tom 'Big Al' Schreiter.
World-renowned Network Marketing Guru   **vii**

Testimonials   **viii**

Introduction   **xii**

About the author   **xiv**

Section 1: Getting Started   **1**

Section 2: Skills   **37**

Section 3: Good Practice   **51**

Section 4: Building Trust   **81**

Section 5: The Big Picture   **93**

Acknowledgements

There will be thousands of people I've forgotten to mention here, who have played a part in my journey, so I apologise in advance.

But I will start by thanking some great mentors – Steve Critchley, for sage advice and helping me grow in my business; Robin Brooks, a great colleague and friend who is always fun to be around; plus Big Al for telling me I should be doing this and then telling me again and again! Art Jonak for his instant friendship and trust and for bringing the network marketing community together worldwide in the way I have tried (with many fine colleagues) to do in the UK. And Randy Gage for inspiring me when I first started in the profession and then helping me when I was given the chance to speak at The Network Marketing Mastermind Event®.

To my Dad for giving me the sheer cheek to think I could do well in this profession. To my Mum for ensuring that I always believed I could succeed right from when I was in a cot. To Cheri and Justin for being wonderful and for giving us our lovely Noah.

To Tristan for his loyal friendship and ongoing encouragement. To Joga for being a great friend and excellent sounding board. To Steve, for the chats, the laughs and the unselfish support. To Jamie for keeping me fit and for being my longest-standing pal! To Mike Burge for badgering me to get this book finished and to focus on the important stuff before it becomes urgent. To Barry the Book for his enthusiasm and support on this project. To Steph for being inspiring. To Jimmy who has provided many lessons for me. To Patricia for the unwavering belief. To the incredible Trainers, Speakers and Leaders I have learnt so much from.

To Malcolm, Wayne, Andrew and Charles who in so many ways made **everything** possible.

To Steve, Joe, Jan (big respect), Andy, Sian, Graeme, Clive, Diana and Alex for their valuable help and feedback.

To all the incredible friends I have made in this profession, all over the world, mainly the distributors I meet from around the globe, irrespective of which company they represent. And of course, to the teammates I have the pleasure of working with and caring for. What a fantastic profession – one that allows us to have fun, enjoy ourselves, help other people and make great money at the same time!

And thanks to my gone-but-not-forgotten great mates Ollie, JohnJo, Clive and Bernell – who in lots of different ways, form part of my journey.

Foreword

What is a compassionate leader? If you were looking for an example of that definition, that person would be Wes Linden. He truly 'leads' – not 'forces' people to become better in their career and in their lives.

One of the definitions of leadership I use is that *"Leaders help people become more in their life, than those people can do on their own."* And this can be done with motivation, inspiration, teaching and ... compassion. Not everyone identifies with the dictator version of leadership, and they are looking for an alternate model.

This book will give simple tasks and insights into how you can get the best out of your new network marketing business and how you can lead your team by simply caring about another person's life and success.

I like the idea of teaching growth, success and leadership with tasks, tips, and clear steps. Too often the big word 'Leadership' sends people off to study lofty principles, theories, and boring, long-winded manuscripts. We all need to be practising leadership before we even learn what it is. Action beats theory every day.

Enjoy putting these 79 tips into practice in your business – starting now.

Tom 'Big Al' Schreiter
www.fortunenow.com

Testimonials

"This is a simple, but highly effective guide to a successful career in network marketing."

Allan Pease
Author of 'Questions are the Answers'

"Wes Linden is one of my favourites. His style is real and conversational and his stories are engaging and relevant. Everyone in our profession will know about this book. Thank you Wes for your dedication, commitment and enthusiasm for the business of network marketing. You are a true gift."

Jordan Adler
Network Marketing Millionaire, Author of 'Beach Money'

"Wes is the new breed of Professional Network Marketer – in his fifteen-year career in the industry he has studied what works and applied it and is still applying it. This is a must-read for any serious network marketing professional."

Barry 'The Book' Phillips
Knowledge Is King

"Packed full of practical advice and written in a straightforward style. Every single one of these tips summarises the secrets of a professional networker and will materially increase your income level."

Andy Waring
Network Marketing Professional and UK Leader

"People wish they could tap into and somehow download the 'brain' of a great leader within the network marketing profession. The great news is, you simply need to read this book because Wes has done that for you. As a tremendous leader within the profession, Wes has mastered a way of thinking in order to be successful in this business and put it all onto paper in a simple and straightforward way. Our advice? Read the entire book immediately. Then, read one tip every single day; journal your thoughts on the idea and proactively start doing it!"

Andrea Waltz & Richard Fenton
Authors of 'Go for No!' and 'Million Dollar Year'

"As a top producer inside the network marketing profession, Wes Linden clearly knows that people prefer simplicity. The simpler you make it, the faster your team will grow. In the spirit of simplicity, Wes shares 79 bite-sized, yet critical 'results-creating' nuggets to help you build a bigger network marketing business. And he does so in a humble, concise, clear and practical way. Truly simple. Bravo!"

Art Jonak
Network Marketing Professional,
Founder of The Network Marketing Mastermind Event®

"Wes is a caring, compassionate leader, coach and mentor helping people win the 'Live First, Work Second' game. With over fifteen years of experience in building a network marketing business Wes has helped thousands of people achieve what he managed to do himself in just five years, by the time he was twenty-four, which was to become non-essential to the creation of his income. This book is packed full of tips and ideas for fast track network marketing success. A must read!"

Chris Williams
Network Marketing Professional,
Author of 'Don't Just Dream It … Do It –
Goal Setting that REALLY works for Network Marketers'

"This book provides the perfect blend of practical tips that make it simple to market and grow a business that is successful and profitable. Follow Wes's advice and watch your profits soar! This book is a must have, and I plan to order a copy for all of my team members."

Lynn Huber
Network Marketing Professional and USA Leader

"Wes Linden is a highly professional and inspirational network marketing leader, whose hard-working approach, warmth and willingness to support his team, have resulted in his current well-earned success. Anyone seeking to follow in his footsteps will find their chances greatly enhanced by reading this book, and following the tips and advice it contains."

The Hon. Charles Wigoder
Executive Chairman of a major
UK Network Marketing Company

"Wes delivers powerful, practical ideas that will instantly boost your bottom line, as well as increase your belief for what is possible in the network marketing profession."

Sarah Robbins
Network Marketing Professional and USA Leader,
Author of 'Rock Your Network Marketing Business'

"What if the best people in the world agreed to sit down with you and tell you what they know? What if Nelson Mandela spoke to you about leadership? Would you take a golf lesson from Tiger Woods? How about if Elton John said he would be your singing coach? If you are committed to making fundamental changes in any area of your life – you should commit to learning from the best.

"For anyone who wants to change their personal finances positively, have fun doing it and still have time for their kids, hobbies and interests – Wes Linden's *79 Network Marketing Tips for Fast-Track Success* is a must read.

"In this remarkable book Wes shares easy-to-understand advice on what he knows best, meaning you are getting guidance from one of the most successful network marketing professionals around."

Barry Duddy
Author of 'Personal Best'

"I had the opportunity to finally hear Wes speak at The Network Marketing Mastermind Event® in Orlando, and he lived up to and blew past his impressive reputation. Few speakers today talk from actual heartfelt experience and authentic truth. This book is a reflection of real work, real struggle and real results. The wise man learns from the experiences of others' and Wes lays down some powerful truths here. Live by them."

Richard Bliss Brooke
Author of 'The Four Year Career' and
'Mach II, The Art of Vision and Self Motivation'

"Wes is a great example of how the future leadership of Network Marketing should be. He focuses and trains on the needs, goals and objectives of the individual – and on the relationships we build, over and above any material or personal income he may gain.

"I say this with absolute authority as I am privileged to have known him as a good friend for the last fifteen years. His first book is a must read for anyone serious about building long-term relationships and a great residual income."

Steve Critchley
Network Marketing Professional and UK Leader

"If you want to fast-track your network marketing business and avoid some of the pitfalls and common mistakes a new distributor can easily mistake, this is the guide for you! Having successfully built a network marketing business myself, I smiled reading this insightful book as Wes has captured the essence of 'what to do' and 'what not to do' in growing an effective and profitable business. It's a must for all new distributors. It is easy to read, simple to understand and clearly laid out. I will certainly be recommending it!"

Carol Sinfield
Network Marketing Professional and UK Leader

"I **love** *79 Network Marketing Tips*! (And I don't remember ever saying **that** before.) Wes Linden claims to be giving reader's 'Insider Tips For Fast Track Success'. That's a classic demonstration of under-promising and over-delivering. What Wes has put together would take most people years – more accurately decades to learn. I've been in this profession for more than 25 years and Wes's *79 Tips* have already taught me things I didn't know – and **need to know**! This is something I want everyone in my business to have a much-used copy of. It's a truly valuable and useful resource. I think it's a Great Book!"

John Milton Fogg
Author of 'The Greatest Networker in the World'

Introduction

Having spent more than fifteen years making lots of errors, mistakes and downright foolish decisions, I felt it was only right to share some of the pitfalls you could easily be snared by in advance of them happening.

In this time, I have built one of the largest and most successful teams with a leading network marketing business, hitting the top positions in that Compensation Plan and become one of the top earners in the network marketing profession.

Along with some great colleagues, I've overseen and pioneered the nationwide training programme for this Company and learnt the value of having a positive, friendly 'everyone is welcome to share and learn' policy to anyone from our profession who wants to succeed, no matter what team, payline or even what network marketing business they are part of.

However, my nature is such that titles and material possessions are less important to me than lifestyle, choices, experiences and the people we choose to share our time with, so helping others succeed is a very important way that I can give back to a profession that has ensured that, after dropping out of university at the age of twenty, I have never had a 'proper' job.

Along the way, I've met thousands upon thousands of good people who have encountered many of the hurdles I discuss in the book, but have not had sufficient guidance or a framework for which to overcome them. **It is time for that to change.**

Within these pages you'll find a collection of the 79 things you **will** come across and how to work your way through them. Why 79? Well, why not 79?!

Don't down tools to read this book! You'll never actually know everything before you start. It's only experience that will actually get you to where you want to be and will help you have a better understanding of the profession we are in. But that doesn't mean I can't give you a heads-up about what may try and bite you.

If you have already got past first base and are starting to build your team, there are **Leaders' Tips** at the end of every bite-sized nugget for you to digest as you start to lead others. If you're a little more advanced with your business-building and you are already leading a fair-sized team, you'll certainly benefit from reading these points, reminding you a little bit of where you were in months or years (or even decades!) gone by when you first started, bringing you face-to-face with the very real issues your new people may be facing.

I wish you well with building your business and hope you'll find this an easy-to-read book which you can pick up and look at time and time again (where different things will make more sense at different stages in your business).

Happy reading! Your friend in the profession,

Wes

PS: Feel free to visit the website for the book:

www.weslinden.com/79tips

*There'll be more tips and resources there – plus a link to my Facebook and Twitter pages should you wish to connect in this way. Be assured, integrity is exceptionally important to me (I am a soccer referee after all, and have officiated within the professional leagues for several years!) and so **only** generic hints and information will be shared with you.*

About the author

Having failed his first year at university, Wes Linden was well on his way to failing his second year too. He had just turned twenty while doing some student teaching as part of his degree, when he first heard about network marketing. Wes was already £10,000 in debt and living with his mother. He'd gone to a good school and his friends were all doing much better than him, on their way to completing medical, legal or economic degrees, and he was pretty directionless.

So he decided to get involved in network marketing to work alongside his studies, in the hope of earning some money in the short term, and building a residual income in the long term. After a few months, Wes was hooked on the network marketing profession and decided to drop out of university ... before he was kicked out!

Although he kept a student mentality (late nights, rubbish TV and parties) he gave his sole focus to his network marketing company and started to make a success of it. Despite many of his friends and peers asking him *"When are you going to get a proper job?"* and suggesting he had been tricked into a scam, Wes rode the storm, and found himself financially semi-retired by the age of 24, and by 27 his residual income had overtaken the average salary of not just a teacher (the career for which he was destined) but a headteacher!

The bare fact is that Wes has never had a 'proper' job thanks to this profession and has only ever been involved with one network. He is still actively involved in his network marketing company as a distributor. In addition, he hosts many of his company's major conventions and presents some of their corporate recruiting videos, while still enjoying building his business as close to the grass roots as possible.

In 2013, Wes was the first ever Brit to speak at the three-day Network Marketing Mastermind Event® in Orlando, alongside the biggest names from the profession in the world. He is vehemently committed to the expansion of the profession and its credibility worldwide and believes this will be simpler when networkers from all companies link arms with each other.

Outside of all this, Wes is a keen-traveller and has on average, one holiday a month. He sees a Personal Trainer at least four times a week, in part to keep fit for his other major interest as a soccer referee where Wes has officiated in the professional leagues up to Championship level for a number of years. He also enjoys spending lots of time with his close friends and family. It's only success in network marketing that has given Wes the choices to do these things whenever he wishes.

☑ **Section 1: Getting Started**

☐ Section 2: Skills

☐ Section 3: Good Practice

☐ Section 4: Building Trust

☐ Section 5: The Big Picture

www.weslinden.com/79tips

Tip 1 Less is more – don't overcomplicate it

One of the biggest challenges for new people (and indeed those who retain the bad habits as they grow within their business), is learning to keep it simple. This is commonly referred to as KISS – Keep It Short & Simple (or Keep it Simple, Stupid!).

The problem is, the typical new distributor is keen, enthusiastic and evangelical about their new business and the products or services. They can't understand why everyone in the world is not doing the business and becoming a consumer!

Add into the mix that they are anxious to get some early successes and bonuses, and this can lead to some very early disappointment.

They bombard their prospect with every piece of information they possess – including (depending on which company you are with):

- the inside leg measurement of the CEO;
- the full lowdown on the technical specification of the pills, potions, creams that they offer;
- the ancient ingredients that can be found in their healthy shake;
- the politics of deregulation in the utility industry, and;
- the potential of the greeting card market!

They think that by telling them about:

- how every bonus works;
- how the residual commission is paid when you've reached the third rung of the ladder;
- the names of the Chairman's children;
- the company's turnover versus ten other companies in the same field.

Then for good measure, they throw in their *"how terrible the real world is"* speech and how the *"pension system is toxic and you are doomed"* talk, and then expect magically to have a new team member desperate to join them!

But the reality? You say too much and **scare off** a perfectly good prospect. They don't get a chance to go onto your 'No for Now' list, in fact you end up on their 'never talk to me again' list!

Plus, even on the off-chance they were remotely interested, what you did is not duplicable and they can't imagine themselves ever being able to do what you did to build their business, so they don't join!

Listen more, say less, don't over-complicate things, keep yourself as someone that people could replicate, and you've got every chance of success!

Leaders' Tip Help your new team members by inviting them to prospect you so that you can hear first-hand whether they are overdoing it. If they are struggling when they are face-to-face with people, either try and go with them on some appointments or ask them to use their phone to record some for you to feedback on.

Tip 2	**Talk to more people – don't hang your hopes on one person**

There's not one single distributor who is bigger than your Company, nor the opportunity. No one person alone can take credit for the creation of the business you represent.

However, I have often seen distributors become obsessed with one individual prospect. It is **not** the end of the world if someone doesn't see the potential **you** do, whether they have yet to join, or even if they have joined. This applies to prospective customers and distributors. Maybe the time isn't right for them yet, but it may well be in the future.

Your network marketing business can continue to grow, with or without that one prospect, and providing you keep talking to people, adding to your pipeline and not fixating on that solitary magic prospect, your business will grow too.

 Leaders' Tip Recognise this in your team members, where they are spending too long on one prospect. I find by asking people about their activity over the past few days you start to realise if they are focusing too much in one place, or likewise if they keep asking you questions about the next plan of attack for the 'sister of my next-door neighbour', you should look to make them conscious, in a polite way of course, of the thousands of other people in their local area and the millions of people in the country!

Tip 3	**Learning to talk about the business at the right time**

If you're looking for a surefire way to lose prospects, confidence, credibility and friends, walk into your local bar and tell a big group of people about your network marketing business. Whether it be about the product, the services, the income opportunity, or all of it, you'll be sure to get shouted down very quickly by know-it-alls.

Fellow network marketers will be quick to label these people as IBEs (Instant Bloody Experts) or GUPTRs (Generally Unsuccessful People Talking Rubbish) – I have also said this – but it doesn't get away from the fact you've just walked into an unnecessary situation which will cost you genuine prospects unless handled differently.

Of course, they don't 'know-it-all' – they just think they do. However, once one starts with their unwelcome feedback, it will become like a bear-baiting tournament. I'm sure you've noticed at a football match, once one or two spectators or players start to jeer the referee, the others join in quickly (as I know only too well from my many enjoyable years as a soccer referee officiating in the professional league, which I still do to this day).

They'll throw every media-driven misconception at you about how the local supermarket's vitamins are better for you than expensive specialist brands; how their telephone company pays **them** to use their phone and broadband; how they get all their home essentials from the 99p shop and not forgetting that Violet and Keith from the post office once used one of those magnetic bracelets and they caught asthma. They'll tell you that pyramid-selling is illegal and that their sister's husband had a cleaner whose next-door neighbour once ended up with a garage-full of water filters and if you're not careful you'll end up with your spare room crammed full of products that no-one wants.

They will pick up your business, toss it around and spew it back at you and you'll be left with no prospects from the exercise, leaving you to continue your gin 'n' tonic with a distinctly bitter taste in your mouth. Depending on how loudly you argue back and defend your decision, they may even resume their 'fun' the next time they see you.

However much they may need the products, opportunity or both, this is simply what happens. They are merely showing off to each other and for some reason a group together in a social or workplace tend to act in this way.

Walking into the bar or the canteen at work as a talking billboard is not the way to do it. These people, described so acerbically (*but believe me, accurately*), are actually probably really decent people and good prospects for your business. But you need to talk to them individually, outside of the pack mentality environment and arrange to see them on their own when they'll behave more like normal, sensible human beings. This means when you are out in these social environments, you can build friendships and relationships with your peer group, which will keep your social life happy and sow seeds for future conversations.

The more questions you can ask people, the more curious you can be about them, the more likely you are to find out their hot buttons and how you can help them, either with your products, opportunity or both.

Now, what do you make of this? A lady I know who is a network marketing distributor, asked for advice on a forum about sending out her wedding invitations with a note attached which said that she and her new husband did not want a gift, but instead everyone should use the money to join her opportunity as a distributor. Naturally, she got several hundred responses suggesting to her that this was a mistake!

Does that story sit right with you? Probably not ... scale this down a bit and it's not that much less palatable than a loud-mouthed stroll into the local bar or canteen where you proclaim to everyone how they must 'BUY BUY BUY' from you.

By the way, if you think I'm exaggerating here and you can buck the trend – give it a go! Let me know how it works, while you lick your wounds at the same time!

 Leaders' Tip Prevent your team from doing this. Too many people will be lost due to shouting too loudly in front of big, rowdy crowds! Ensure they know what is appropriate and where they are better-placed to simply build relationships and grow their friendships.

Tip 4 Motivation doesn't last long

Think of how many careers involve years of study and how long you had to train to do what you do now, whether it be in formal education, courses, or learning on the job. So don't be surprised that those who make a real success of their network marketing business re-attend the training that is on offer more than once every five years! Sometimes, it is to accompany a new team member, other times it is simply for a refresher.

Just like watching a good film again, you will always spot things you hadn't seen the first time, or indeed you may see things differently based on the experiences you have had since the previous training.

Plus, you'll benefit from hearing a different spin from other Leaders and meeting local distributors who you may be able to buddy-up or swap tips with.

When you are at these events ensure you take good notes – it is better to have a short pencil than a long memory! Where necessary (and allowed) use your phone to record some of the speakers.

I appreciate that in some network marketing businesses, cross-networking still has a way to go in terms of becoming part of the culture, but I can only stress how valuable I believe this to be in truly ensuring that the business grows in the right way. I like to think of every distributor in 'my' Company (irrespective of whether they're in my pay-line or not) as being part of the same team, not as the competition – we all have the same goal and by the Company succeeding, we all succeed. Think of 'TEAM' as meaning:

Together **E**veryone **A**chieves **M**ore

Nearly everyone who re-attends training reports how they feel invigorated and re-motivated too, and the association with others from the entire organisation can make a real difference.

 Leaders' Tip Teams need to be led. Ensuring you are always reminding your team of when the next training sessions are and getting them buddying up with other distributors at the events and car-sharing, will allow them to swap ideas and experiences with their peers.

Tip 5 Understanding the Personality Types

Many of us will have developed great people skills over many years of walking the planet. However, perhaps more than any other type of business, in this profession you'll be exposed to every type of personality – and to be a real success it would be valuable for you to be able to quickly identify how you are going to best relate to those you are doing business with. The different types of personality can be split into four colours and explained from there – it is not just educational but also very enlightening.

Network marketing legend Tom 'Big Al' Schreiter has recorded a CD set on understanding *Colours* called: *How to Speak The Secret Language of Your Prospects*, available from his website www.fortunenow.com, it is well worth listening to. If you have not spent time either listening to or reading any of Big Al's stuff, you have missed out.

I certainly found the simple *Colours* formula to have been a real help when interacting with the huge assortment of people that make our profession so fulfilling.

 Leaders' Tip Simple skills such as *Colours* are important for you to understand, not only for when you are dealing with different types of people in your business, but also to help those in your team who perhaps struggle to understand that a 'one-size-fits-all' approach is not going to bring them the results they desire.

Tip 6   It can be lonely ... or fun!

There have been many people with perfectly sound businesses, who have suffered the curse of self-employed loneliness! While working for yourself is a dream come true for many, if you are used to social interaction and you like the buzz of being around people, settling in to a new way of working can be difficult for some if they don't have others around to banter with or to share experiences and stories.

Even though most people starting out in our profession will still have another job or business, this may not always satisfy the need for contact with others when building their network marketing empire.

Therefore, be sure to attend the trainings as well as the opportunity presentations, the company social events and team meetings, as often as you can. Use the distributor online forums and buddy-up with those local to you to ensure you have regular input with others, you can exchange hints and tips, get frustrations off your chest and make new friends. Keep positive to ensure your journey is fun, rather than laborious.

Embrace these opportunities and it is a wonderful climb to the top of the mountain, shared with others who help, encourage and motivate you.

 Leaders' Tip Team socials, coffee mornings and buddying people up will contribute towards satisfying your new team member's desire for a regular dose of interaction and positive association.

Tip 7   Building a **big** list

On your first training or first meeting with your sponsor, there will doubtless be list-building exercises to help you with a plan as to who to contact at first. You'll be encouraged to add everyone you know to that list.

By the time we reach the age of eighteen, we know at least 500 people by name, who know us too. We may not realise it, but we do.

Think about it – ex-school pals, ex-teachers, ex-neighbours, former work colleagues, friends of the family, golfing friends, gym buddies, the list is endless.

Here is a method I have used to help with memory jogging, for many years. It's a tried and trusted favourite called FROGS:

F	R	O	G	S
Friends and family	**Recreational contacts**	**Occupational contacts**	**Geographical contacts**	**Same name contacts**
This bit should be self-explanatory. Don't forget old friends you've lost touch with; it's a great excuse to get back in touch! Old school friends, old neighbours, old work colleagues. They don't have to be old! Who attended your wedding?	Who do you play sports with? Who do you socialise with? Who do you come into contact with when you socialise? e.g. barmen, restauranteurs? People who take money from you? Who attends your church? Who works with charities that you support?	Who do you work with? Who do you come into contact with as a result of work? Reps, accountants, sales assistants, people from other departments? People who supply you with products to help you in your business? People who earn money from you?	Who do you deal with that lives a long way away? Who do you call that is a national call (check your phone bill)? Who do you know who lives over 50 miles away from you? Who do you know that lives in a place where there's a famous sports team, e.g. New York, Chelsea, Manchester, Barcelona, Milan?	Go back through your list, and try and think of people who have the same name as people who you have now written down. Who has the same name as you, your mum and dad, your brothers and sisters? Who do you know whose name begins with A? B? C? D? E? F? etc.

Where people fall down when it comes to list-building, is by omitting some acquaintances. Here's a suggestion – if you can think of their name, include it on your list. You may not have seen them for thirty years, but add them anyway. You may have no idea how you are going to get in touch with them – but you should still add them.

Here's an additional memory jogger that you can use:

Who do you know that ...

are members of the Parent Teacher Association?	**works** under great pressure?
	I respect?
are my babysitter's parents?	**did** my plumbing?
are the parents of my children's friends?	**rewired** my house?
are the people I met on holiday?	**painted** my living room?
cleans my clothes?	**is** considered a leader?
helps in the garden, or around the house?	**has** blonde hair? Or ginger hair? Or no hair?!
deals with the public?	**is** ambitious?
works in the police, fire, postal service, etc.?	**has** just graduated from college or university?
does personal counselling?	
is a religious leader?	**is** in a management or supervisory capacity?
has children just starting school?	**is** in the Lions, Rotary, WI, Masons?
has just bought a new house?	**is** retired but active?
has talents but is held back?	**wants** more out of life?
is a Teacher? Doctor? Solicitor? Accountant?	**is** my boss?
who designed my house or conservatory?	**runs** their own business?
is an experienced salesman?	**is** the most successful person I know?
works in a bank?	**will** help me to succeed?
manages a shop?	**has** pension worries?
owns or runs a taxi service?	**runs** a printing business?
relies on ideas for a living (e.g. authors, designers, promoters, advertisers)?	**sells** ice cream or runs a van?
	shows respect for and cares for other people?
services my car?	**wants** freedom?
has failed in business but wants to succeed?	**is** saved in my mobile phone?

Why do I say to add everyone you can think of? Firstly, building a massive list psychologically helps you to realise you have a lot of people to contact. If you have got five people on your list, and one says 'no' – 20% of your potential business is gone! But if you have five hundred people on your list and one says 'no' – you still have 99.8% of your list to approach!

Secondly, the mind and the universe have a funny way of bringing us into contact with people we have not seen for a while when we add them to our list. How? It's not actually magic – it just means your senses are heightened to that person and if you walk past them in the shopping centre, you're more tuned in to recognise them, when you may have otherwise not noticed their smile, voice or eyes through the crowd.

Thirdly, when you come across someone who was previously a mutual contact of yours and a contact you haven't seen for a long time, you get a little jolt to the memory-box and hear a voice saying: *"Ask about whether they've seen Peter recently"* or: *"Ask if they know what Shannon is up to now."*

Even if they don't know and haven't heard from them for a while either – guess what? – weeks later they may spot them on Facebook in someone else's wedding photos, or may bump into an old acquaintance who knows the mystery friend.

None of this is to say you should instantly start 'selling' the business opportunity or product and services to your old acquaintance when you catch up with them again – no – you need to build a relationship with them, find out where they're at and – who knows? – they could be in the right place to hear what you have to offer. If not, stay in touch and not only might you rekindle an old friendship, but you'll be in the vicinity when the time is right for them to consider what your business offers.

 Leaders' Tip Ask to see your team member's list. Let them see yours (it better be big!) and help them expand on the names they currently have already. The list is never actually big enough. You can spend a whole hour or more doing this every time you see them, using FROGS and whatever other imaginative stuff you can think of! Do not allow people to rely on iPhones, laptops, spreadsheets or databases – they need a simple and duplicable list that they can share with their team when it grows (and if their team doesn't grow, it means they don't have a big enough list!).

Tip 8 — Don't be afraid of the big wide world that's out there

As discussed already, we probably know around 500 people by name by the time we are eighteen. If each of them introduced us to ten other people via referrals (also discussed in more detail in Tip 9) then that's 5000 people. Now, if we continue pushing this equation, it wouldn't take long to cover the whole of the country!

However, taking a more pragmatic approach to the maths, even if you only take the 500 people you know personally, there's still another 59,999,500 people (or so) in the UK who you **don't** know (or lots, lots more in Europe or the USA if your business operates in these areas).

That's a big target market! So, if you want to expand beyond your warm market to top-up your prospecting pipeline into a more cold market, this is not a difficult thing to do. Whether this be through networking events, team-organised events at local county shows, fêtes, boot sales and fairs, making personal contact with those in your street and the surrounding districts, postcards in the shops around your area, wearing an attention-grabbing badge, speaking to people when you're out and about, utilising permitted online and social media opportunities, chatting to local fellow business owners ... the sky is the limit and there really is no reason why you should ever feel there's no-one to speak to.

It's also really important not to prejudge the outcome or someone's likelihood of saying 'yes' based on how you find them when you meet them – for example, they may seem a little down or lacking in spark, but maybe it's a bad day, or they're not enjoying their job, or they're deep in thought, or something is wrong at home. Until you smile and open up the conversation, you'll never know.

One thing some people tend to find more advantageous in the cold arena is that the people you are talking to do not already know you as a carpenter, shop worker, teacher or mum, hence you may not have to overcome that mental stumbling block that can psychologically hinder (unnecessarily in my opinion) some folk.

Here's a thought for you – network marketing is about networking!

Next time the local distributor from one of the catalogue-based businesses puts something through your door – or you see a card in a shop window for another network marketing business, why not change your thinking on your approach for this, from desperately trying to recruit them from their business into yours, into thinking more professionally.

This person isn't bait, or a target – they are a network marketing colleague. The tens of millions of people who aren't network marketing distributors for a company in your country are your targets.

So, why not pop an order in for something useful from their offering, with a note saying *"Hey – thanks for the catalogue – I always like to support other network marketers. If you fancy a coffee some time to chat and see if we can learn some tips and share some local contacts, then here's my phone number 07123 456789, Best wishes, Jamie."*

You might find that person becomes a **far** more valuable contact for you than trying to just leave them with your card, DVD and opportunity brochure!

Whatever your approaches, these can end up costing you money. Consider reinvesting your profits from your network marketing business or be sure to have a set budget which isn't going to see you going hungry the following week.

The key is, always be open to other ways of increasing your list – but be sure to take advice from those more senior in the business as to what has worked and what hasn't, to save yourself some time.

 Leaders' Tip Even if the cold market isn't your favoured route, it may work for some people and if they **want** to try it, guide them as best you can or put them in touch with people who have had success in that area. I don't believe any of this should mean people completely ignore their warm market.

Tip 9   Getting referrals

Every time you put in some effort to generate a customer appointment, that is, of course, a most productive use of time. But imagine if every moment you were spending time trying to generate customer appointments, you were actually **in** a customer appointment?

There is only really one way this is possible and that's by ensuring you become competent at generating referrals. Mastering the art of collecting qualified customer referrals, in which you engage the customer in helping you secure an appointment, is a terrific way to maximise your time and ensure that you are sitting in front of people who have already been part-sold to by a friend or family member of their own who they know, like and trust – making your job simpler. A few names and phone numbers on a piece of paper handed to you by a new customer, if they haven't 'warmed them up', is only one step advanced from selecting random numbers from the phone book.

There's an easy way and a hard way to keep your pipeline full of potential customers waiting to see you. The easy way is to master referrals and practice on every customer! Do this by taking advice from those in your business who are proving themselves excellent at gathering referrals with your products. Ensure you expose yourself to some advanced referral training (plus any books or CDs on the subject) and being vigilant in practising it, is sage advice if you are looking to make sure customer acquisition is a stroll in the park for you.

What about the hard way? Well, just don't ask anyone for referrals and consistently seek out new customers. I'd go for the easy route if I were you!

 Leaders' Tip Master referrals yourself and this will make it easier to teach. A team full of people who are competent at getting referrals will grow the business much quicker.

Tip 10 Go upline beyond your sponsor

Be in no doubt, your sponsor will be a loyal and encouraging force for good – I have no hesitation in believing that the person who introduced you has every positive intention for your success.

However, depending on the extent to which they have exposed themselves to the business up to this point, and how experienced they are, they may not always be best-placed to guide you. You should be able to make a judgment on this yourself.

Moreover, your sponsor may have goals that are very real to them, but are not as ambitious as your own – or indeed vice versa. This doesn't make these goals any more or less valid, but just personal to the individual, which may well mean you want to work at a different pace or have other intentions when it comes to your approach.

This is a really good reason to ensure that you have contact with other members of your upline team. It is very much in their interest to help you succeed, so be sure to use them. Try and interact with, and introduce yourself, to as many of the team as possible – no matter how 'high up' you think they are. You never know who you will have the most synergy with. Either your sponsor or your Head Office support team can put you in touch.

How about finding a 'Success Buddy'? Someone at a similar level to you with matching aspirations for whom you make yourself accountable and likewise they do the same with you. It could be someone in your team, your upline, or from a completely different part of the business. It could even be someone from another network, providing the business intentions of both parties is entirely honourable.

Cross-networking with other distributors outside of your team is something I highly recommend – when people help each other from a position of good intention rather than *"I'm going to earn from this"*, it's a very pure and authentic relationship and builds a great culture in your business and in our profession.

Leaders' Tip As a Leader, you should be making a welcome phone call to every new distributor in your team, and encourage all others in the sponsorship line to do the same to each new person. There are so many benefits to this:

- a different voice who they can create synergy and rapport with;
- tips and advice;
- helps the new person feel a sense of belonging and part of something special;
- makes them realise there's plenty of support and a totally different working environment to anything they've experienced before.

I think this approach increases retention considerably and it is something I have used and taught regularly in my business and when speaking abroad.

One thing you'll come to realise is that your superstars can come from anywhere – and 'every dud knows a stud' so you need to have a handle on who is joining so you can get to know the future Leaders from day one.

As a Leader, encourage cross-networking with other people outside of the team – this is one way that people really can grow. Of course, once your new team member has a group that starts growing beyond their own efforts, the chances are **they** will duplicate these early welcome calls which will be great for your business in the long term.

Tip 11 | Your personal development

People join this type of business with many varied, rich and interesting backgrounds. However, in many cases they are looking to make some changes and improvements to their lifestyle, which could lead us to assume that not everything has gone 100% to plan up to this point. This is not a criticism, simply an assumption based on many years' experience in this profession, and I appreciate it won't be true in every case.

I'm treading sensitively here because the next bit can shock some people! When you arrive into your new network marketing business, it is very likely that the personal development you have invested in and the mindset you have, may need topping up or tweaking – that is as kindly as I can put it!

Basically, you are wherever you are right now, as a result of the decisions you've made and the attitude you have. If this has not entirely brought you the output you were hoping for, then some things need to change and what is absorbed in your mind will make a real difference.

People spend a lot of money on their car – servicing, improving, cleaning inside and out. They spend lots of money on their hair with regular visits to their stylist or barber and using products daily. This can work out to be quite expensive when you add it all up! However, some people will baulk at the thought of spending the same on a book or CD (that will help their mindset and attitude to ensure they are in the right place to build this type of business in their spare time) as they spend on their smoking habit. This can't be right!

If you are teachable and open-minded to learning, if you realise you don't know everything about succeeding in your network marketing business just yet, and that the wheel has been turning for many years and doesn't need to be reinvented, you can truly build a business and income as big as you choose.

Even reading just ten pages of a book each day will mean over the course of a year, you have read over 3500 pages that will probably amount to around twenty-five to thirty-five books! If I told you to read twenty-five books in the next twelve months, you would probably think you wouldn't have time – but ten pages a day is very achievable.

Both Darren Hardy, in his book and CD set *The Compound Effect* and Jeff Olson in his excellent book and CD, *The Slight Edge*, recommend this very same principle.

I have yet to meet anyone who has done well in any network marketing business, who has not engaged in personal development, whether it be books, CDs, events or a combination of all three. I just don't believe we arrive in this profession equipped to get to the top with what the school education system has taught us – and to which the conventional job market has conditioned us.

My top tip for you is to ask what is the favourite personal development book or CD of those who have achieved what you are looking to emulate – and then get it! If you can find time to read, for example, five of your ten pages a day, first thing in the morning, and then the other five before you go to sleep, you really are setting your day up well, while sending yourself to sleep in a positive frame of mind. CDs are also great for the car journey to and from work, plus technology means you can download audios and have them on your phone or iPod for listening to on the train, when at the gym or walking the dog.

One thing I believe every person who is looking to be successful should do in order to ensure they get a guaranteed monthly fix of personal development is to join the *Knowledge is King 'Book of the Month'* club. You get the latest and hottest new-release book or CD sent direct, often before it is freely available to the general public. Postage and packing is free and it costs around the same as a cinema ticket each month. For more details go to www.knowledgeisking.co.uk. For those outside the UK, check with your upline team to see if there are similar subscription opportunities available.

Ultimately, unless you're a footballer, a dancer or an artist, we are all minimum wage workers from the neck down, so whatever you can do to develop your mindset, attitude and thinking can only benefit you as you strive for success.

Oh, and if you're one of the people who says: *"I don't need that mumbo-jumbo stuff"* – then you definitely need it!

Leaders' Tip In the earliest days when new distributors may not realise the value of this input, lend them a book or CD of your own. Indeed, if you have your own small library and you get people started this way (keep a note of who borrows what though), you'll find it won't be long before they start investing in these materials themselves and then when they start to build their team, they'll do the same!

Tip 12   Start your own 'list books' <u>today</u>

When we start, we tend to believe that every single person is going to see what we see as enthusiastically as we see it, and that they'll just jump immediately on-board. Sorry to break it to you, but this won't always be the case!

Indeed, often those you think will join straight away, don't; and those who you think wouldn't be interested, are! The only thing I can tell you after all these years in this profession about who I know will join, is that I **don't** know.

The important thing is to remain friends with them, say to them: *"That's okay, but would it be okay if I keep you updated with how it's all going?"* Not one person has ever responded to me with a 'no' here! This keeps the door open for you to talk to them again in the future and at some stage the time may be right for them to take a proper look at what you are offering.

For this reason, I believe from day one you should have a special book labelled 'No for Now' (or 'Yes for Later' if you prefer) and that whenever you speak to someone and they either say *"no thanks"* or *"not right now"* or *"maybe later"* or *"it's not something I would be interested in"* or even that you don't actually get a response from them on the matter, you add them to this book with any notes that will remind you of their situation and what they have seen, or not yet seen.

In his excellent book and CD *Beach Money*, Jordan Adler explains how he has two list books – he has his equivalent of a 'No for Now' book, which has a green cover. He also has a book with a black cover and this is his list of people he has yet to speak to about his business.

Those who have, up to this point turned down (or just not said 'yes' to) the business go in the green book. Why green? Green is the colour of money (in the USA!) and so he calls it his 'Money Book'. This is the most valuable list you will have.

The way I have always used my 'No for Now' book is that every time there is a positive press article about the business, an improvement to a product or the opportunity, or a great new incentive, I would go through my book and contact those people for whom the news I have may strike a chord and simply tell them: *"I just thought I would keep you up-to-date with how the business is going, as I promised I would"* and always ensure, once I have told them the information or sent them the link, I don't let the conversation finish without asking: *"So, is now a better time for you to take another look to see how the business can benefit you?"*

Your 'No for Now' book will actually be worth a lot more to you in the long term than your list of people you haven't yet spoken to. There are many, many success stories about people who have taken weeks, months or even years to join the business but go on to make a real impact. If they had been deleted from someone's list and never had the business mentioned to them again, they would never have been able to rewrite their life story by being given the chance to make changes that another forty years in the conventional job market would not offer them.

One of the most profitable legs in my own team came from one of the many people who I have kept in contact with for years on end – in this particular case, ten years was how long it took for the timing to be right for him to join.

The same principle applies to those becoming customers, the timing has to be right for them.

Start your list books right away and keep adding to them!

 **Leaders' Tip** Being a Leader means having a Leader's vision well into the future and realising that this is a longer term plan than just your first few conversations. Ensure that you keep your own lists in this manner and have your own 'No for Now' book (in green if you want) and let your team see this. The more they see you do, the more they are likely to emulate.

Jordan Adler keeps it as simple as the black and green book so it passes his 'Eight Year Old Test', in that anything he does or teaches has to be so simple that an eight year old can do it – this is something to live by yourself.

Tip 13 Prejudging costs you money

This is a topic for every person who tells me: *"yeahhh but you don't know Neil"* or *"Ruth wouldn't be interested"*. I can give you countless examples of people who were prejudged (or could easily have been so) but who have joined and are now growing successful businesses.

From students to teachers, actors to sportspeople, police officers to judges, shop workers to labourers, millionaires to paupers, business owners to those who have never found their place in life, the unemployed to reformed alcoholics; you name it, these people have succeeded in our profession.

In fact, the only thing I **do** know about who will or won't succeed or who will or won't join, is that I **don't** know – and that is after nearly two decades in the profession.

A few years ago in my network marketing business, a seasoned and experienced distributor decided to take me on my word about not prejudging and so he asked every single customer who he had signed up, without fail, to look at the business opportunity with him. Irrespective of whether they were, in his opinion very wealthy or too old, it didn't matter, he mentioned the opportunity.

He conducted this experiment with over 200 customers. Of them, around thirty-five became distributors. Now, my network marketing business is not one whereby customers become a distributor in order to get a preferential price on their purchase – they generally only become a distributor if they are serious about building an additional income. So, this meant his ratio was around one in seven. Some people will have a far better ratio, others will have far worse. But as Jim Rohn says, you need to find **your** ratio and then work on improving it.

His conclusion to this exercise was summed up rather well when he said to me: *"I just asked every one of them – I didn't let anyone scupper my stats – I realised that if I had prejudged them and made decisions for them, I would never have got it right. So I calculated if I had only asked the thirty-five I thought were most suitable, I would not have got it right and my ratio would still have been 1 in 7 therefore I would have ended up with only five new distributors out of those 200 customers."*

It was his closing words that really hit home: *"It's not my role to play God with people's lives – I have something that is of benefit, my job is to offer it to them and it's up to them whether they want to take it further."*

Don't prejudge and you'll never get it wrong.

 Leaders' Tip Always be sure to check with your new distributors whether they mentioned the opportunity when they are letting you know the good news about their latest customer sale!

Tip 14 Relax! Some people say 'No'!

This is one I can keep short and sweet – and deliberately so.

Some people will say 'no' – it's part of the process – understand that, embrace it, accept it and relax!

Add them to your 'No for Now' list, remain friends, keep in contact and who knows what will happen in the future.

Listen to and read the enlightening *Go for No*, by Richard Fenton and Andrea Waltz. This will really help you learn to understand how to process the 'no' word.

Keep the 4SW principle in mind:

- Some Will,

- Some Won't,

- So What,

- Someone's Waiting!

 Leaders' Tip Help your team members understand this, keep their spirits high when it happens and you'll grow a great business!

Tip 15 Breathe more when you speak!

Ever been to a car showroom or to look at a new television and had a sweet, but geeky salesperson, literally panting with excitement at a potential sale – so much so they can barely get their words out?

It's a little off-putting and it puts the customer very firmly in the driving seat. In fact, if you watch this scenario from a safe distance you'll see that customers can almost enjoy the chance to push the buttons of a submissive and desperate sale-seeker.

This is a stance to avoid at all costs! Make sure when you speak to someone about the business, whether they have shown some curiosity to begin with, or you are just in the throes of cultivating their interest, you do so calmly and with posture. If you are trying to get out so many words in the hope of pressing their hot button, you'll likely put them off and appear desperate.

Moreover, while the prospect is asking themselves if they could do this, your breathless rambling is telling them that they wouldn't want to be doing the same and so perhaps the business opportunity isn't going to be for them.

Smile ... relax ... posture ... breathe!

 Leaders' Tip Keep your team focused on the long term, and mindful that not everyone is going to say (or needs to say) 'yes' the first time they're spoken to. Remind your team members to remain relaxed and to breathe properly and this will increase their odds of introducing those prospects they are talking to.

Tip 16 Do business with people who do business with you

This is a relatively simple one but I love it. You are now a business owner, nothing less! A very sound practice is to attempt only to do business with people that do business with you. That means exercising your right to choose where you spend your money!

I am not saying other business owners don't have the right to say 'no' to your offering, however, if they are completely closed to you even showing them, or they get funny with you when you tell them, there are undoubtedly plenty more people in their field who would love you to spend money with them instead.

Cleaners, gardeners, dentists, opticians, mechanics, builders, conservatory blind sellers and many more have all gone by the wayside because they weren't even **prepared** to have the discussion (those who have met me will know that my hairdresser had to go for other reasons!). They didn't have to say 'yes' – but they just needed to give me the respect of listening to what I had to say.

One builder even queried with me why he had seen another builder's van outside my house doing some work, which allowed me the satisfaction of telling him why I had given £5,000 of work to someone else! I'm mean ...

Take this posture and approach with those that you do business with and you'll find no end of prospects to talk to.

 Leaders' Tip Basic practices like this will ensure your team members are 'walking the walk' and proud of the Company (and profession) you both represent – work with them to ensure they are conscious of this area of warm lists and be certain they talk to them about their business.

Tip 17 | Confusing residual income with wages

This is a common problem in the early days. This is your own business and like all new businesses it takes time to get off the ground and build up. It doesn't mean it doesn't work, it means you are laying the foundations for future success and prosperity.

Here's the problem though – over the course of the month, you may go to a training for a day; do four of five presentations of which some say 'yes', some say 'no'; have a couple of afternoons making calls and doing follow-ups; watch a few training videos online; or take a guest along to one of the Opportunity Presentations. However, you will only actually get paid for product sales to customers, plus any team-building bonuses you are due, plus the residual commission generated by the volume spend of your personal or group customers in the previous month (this will all vary from Company to Company).

You do not receive an hourly wage nor do you get a payment for the seeds you've planted and the time put in. This is where some people fall down, as they may feel somewhat despondent because of what they may perceive to be a time-to-reward imbalance. However, this is where the big money is made! You lay foundations and you plant seeds that in the future will pay big dividends.

The key is to remember that, at times you may feel 'underpaid' initially; but without going through this building period you will not get to the stage where **you** become inconsequential to the creation of your income.

I remember looking at a name on a commission statement once and thinking *"It's ten years since I introduced that person ... that means I have been paid 120 times on that initial half hour I spent with them!"*

This applies to introducing customers and when you spend time helping a new distributor ... once they start building volume and introducing their own team you never actually stop getting paid for the efforts of all of those involved – that's a very cool place to be! This is where you truly become unimportant to how much income you receive.

Whatever you do, don't look at a commission statement and think *"I did all that work for this?"* – if you do, you have failed to understand the real beauty of residual income and you may find you never truly get benefit from it.

Leaders' Tip Do you really understand the true value of residual income? If not, try taking three months off work – without notice and don't mention it to your boss and see how much you earn from your conventional job! It's vital that you help your team understand this because nobody who truly understands the magic of residual income will ever quit your business.

Tip 18 | Don't be a secret agent!

"Ssshhh ... whatever you do, don't tell anybody about your new business!"

When did anyone say this to you? At what training was it explained to you that people will be able to guess about how you can help them improve their lives with your product or service offering and your opportunity?

Being a secret agent – or 'being in the network marketing closet', is one of the biggest early killers of the business.

Quite simply, if people don't know how you can help them, they can't say 'yes'. They're certainly not going to come and ask you if they don't know to do so.

This doesn't mean religiously chanting it wherever you go. It just means you should ensure you mention it to people as and when you speak to them or at the very least sow a seed for the future.

If you don't have business cards in your wallet or bag along with a prospecting tool (could be a DVD, CD, opportunity pack), plus prospecting tools in the car and by the front door, then you're a secret agent.

It isn't always the right moment to tell people, but as long as they find out at some stage, there's a much greater chance they will say 'yes'.

 Leaders' Tip It's another very basic but major killer of businesses – you need to ensure your team are not keeping their great new business a secret, otherwise they can come to all the meetings, buy all the books, but they'll never progress.

Tip 19 — Doing a lot sporadically versus a little bit consistently

Something to be cautious of is peaking too quickly, and then fading away. I see this many times. Likewise, I often see people who dip in and out frequently; for example, when they're on form, they're everywhere – at all the training sessions and opportunity presentations; and generally making a loud noise. Then, something happens and they disappear for a period of time.

Obviously, other commitments can be a factor in this, which is of course, how life goes sometimes.

But if your intention is to make a success of your network marketing business and your other commitments allow for you to keep your focus even if it is just in your spare time, then you should attempt to ensure you do what you can **consistently**, rather than doing a lot sporadically and then losing your momentum.

World-renowned network marketing speaker and thought leader Randy Gage puts this into perspective when he talks about people who say that their network marketing business is taking up too much of their spare time. He says that it is actually your job that takes up too much of your spare time (forty to fifty hours per week) and that it's your network marketing business which will one day allow you to have some of that time back. This is a useful mindset shift for people who can't find consistency and use time as the excuse.

 Leaders' Tip It's important to have empathy with your team members in terms of their other commitments and not come across as a bully. It's their business at the end of the day! However, when you notice them blowing hot and cold it is important for you to get an understanding of what is going on, whether there's problems at home or work, and if you can help. Your support for them extends beyond just answering product questions and when you show them you care, you'll never lose them.

Remember, people don't care how much they know, until they know how much you care.

Tip 20 | Giving out leaflets and brochures and expecting a result

If the way to big numbers is simply handing out leaflets and brochures, then why does your network marketing company need you?

One of the big challenges I see is when people join and hand out hundreds of leaflets and expect the phone to ring! They get a nasty surprise when that doesn't happen.

This isn't because the products and services aren't worthy or because people don't want them. It's because the products, services and opportunity are best shared by an enthusiastic voice rather than by reams of documentation or leafleted marketing messages. At the very least, if you are going to hand out brochures willy-nilly, or drop leaflets in the local area (and I don't advise this as your main mode of attack) then be sure to follow up by going back to people and asking them: *"What did you like best?"* The network marketers in the catalogue-sales businesses would also see a much greater uptake by asking that (or a similar) question when they collect back their materials from their prospects.

Never forget: people buy people – this will never change ...

 Leaders' Tip Whenever a team member mentions they are off to hand out some paraphernalia, be sure to check with them how they are doing with their own warm list and referrals. They may be in need of some extra coaching or support.

Tip 21   Comparisons versus big picture

No matter what type of products or services you offer, there are likely to be competitors and imitators that can be found somewhere or other. This means there are other price points or tariffs that you will find available, sometimes cheaper, sometimes more expensive. So, it is feasible from time to time that you will spot other 'deals' in the marketplace and you will also probably notice competitors much more frequently now you are a distributor than when you weren't so alert.

No doubt if you have done your research properly, you are part of a company which has a great value offering, with fantastic customer service (including **you** as part of the after-sales care) top accolades from independent sources, an unchallengeable track record and brilliant credibility. How can I say that? Network marketing businesses that last really do need to stand out if they are relying on people like you to put their credibility on the line and recommend them.

Competitors offer what they offer! Focus on your proposition rather than dissecting the competition (especially when you are talking to prospects who have not even asked about competitors) as this will keep you on track to the big picture rewards that are available within the profession.

Leaders' Tip Look out for the analytical types who spend too long trying to cover every eventuality and have a spreadsheet of every single competitor tariff or product offering – they are non-duplicable and are likely to blow out all prospects who are not analysers (which will be the majority). They will think that just because they might like finer detail, that everyone is the same. How many people really know exactly what their mortgage rate is or the miles per gallon their car does? If people don't know these details, are they really likely to want to know every iota of comparative analysis on your products or services? Coach them to understand that by focusing on benefits rather than features, and leading with their personality, they are likely to have more widespread appeal.

Tip 22 Edit your income

This is a pretty simple one. Sorry, but it's one you'll not be able to buck, however smart or perceptive you think you are.

Every time you pass up an opportunity to talk to someone about the business, deciding for yourself that it wouldn't be right for them, or that they wouldn't be interested, you have edited your income.

People will read this comment and think: "*Yeah, but what if they're not interested and I am right?*" – to this I say that you may well be right on an occasional, isolated basis. You may even be right more times than you are wrong. However, what if you are wrong 10% of the time? If you pass up speaking to ten people a fortnight as you thought you knew that they wouldn't join, of whom one **would** have joined, that's two people per month you deny the opportunity to benefit from your products or services, make money, or both. Twenty-four potential distributors and/or customers per year.

To make matters worse, if they each only gave you two referrals on average, there are another forty-eight people you've missed out on!

Don't get me started on how the numbers would exponentially explode if they were all distributors – even working on small averages, you would be missing out on significant numbers in your team. A very expensive mistake. You have essentially edited your income, even though you might have been correct 90% of the time. The outcome of this is unseen in reality, because it's pretty difficult to conceptualise the ifs, buts and maybes. Many years experience in this business tells me that I am right!

This can sometimes manifest itself graphically when you see one of those people you chose *not* to ask at a Company event having joined with someone else! You'll probably even notice an unpleasant, queasy feeling when you see them being presented and lauded on stage as a newly-promoted achiever.

Many people express surprise that the people they expect to say 'yes', say 'no', and those that say 'no' are the ones who they thought would be interested. There are many examples of customers who join months or years later with a different distributor to the one who showed them the products initially, quite simply because they did not know about the opportunity from their initial contact.

The worse that can happen is that someone says: *"No thanks, not for me"* and you can pop them on your 'No for Now' list as discussed previously. This also ensures they'll never then be able to say: *"Why didn't you tell me about this?"* years down the track.

Don't get caught out – be sure to let everyone know what you do and offer them the chance to take a look – that way you'll not be kicking yourself in the future.

 Leaders' Tip This is a really important message and one you should be sure to point out to your team. You won't ever win with this point, no matter how much you tell yourself you're right, there will always be one that catches you out and luck will doubtless mean that when it does catch you out, it'll be a costly mistake!

Tip 23 | Understand early bonuses

There will be a fair bit to take in when you join, but apart from the obvious up-front bonuses that your plan may offer, which you should most certainly understand how to qualify for, there may well be other promotions that are running that you are able to benefit from.

These vary from time to time, from Company to Company, but be sure to check with your Leaders and to be safe, with Head Office, whether there are holiday, share option, car, iPad or other incentives, as it is always a shame when people miss out on opportunities they could have qualified for if only they'd had time to prepare.

 Leaders' Tip The smart Leader will be one step ahead with this, ensuring their new folk are given as much incentive as possible to get started.

☑ Section 1: Getting Started

☑ **Section 2: Skills**

☐ Section 3: Good Practice

☐ Section 4: Building Trust

☐ Section 5: The Big Picture

Tip 24 | Silent idiot

One of the ways I see people alienate their prospects is by unintentionally calling them an 'idiot', but doing so silently. What am I talking about?!

For example, you are either prospecting someone or talking to them during an appointment and you ask them:

"So where do you get your supplements currently?"

To which the person replies: *"The supermarket"*.

Then, with a slightly high-pitched and inquisitive voice you say:

"The suuuuuupermarrrrkettt?"

Or maybe you're in the utilities industry and you ask:

"So who do you use for your energy?"

To which they respond: *"Super Power"*.

That similarly-toned squeal follows as you say:

"Suuuuuuppppperrrrrr Powerrrrrrr?"

Without realising it you have just called them an 'idiot'. You have intimated they must be stupid to have made that decision. In criticising their previous choice, they are likely to become defensive and feel the need to justify that it wasn't a stupid choice and now you're into a battle. Chances are, they'll not consider what you have to say out of principle.

Had you not responded that way, you had a better chance of **them** telling **you** why their previous choice was not a great one.

It's the same when talking about the business opportunity. You say to someone: *"So what is it you're doing now?"* and they explain *"Oh, I'm working at Jones's Coffee Shop now."*

What follows is that slight screech and an up-turn in your voice towards the end of the word as you patronisingly say: *"Jooooonnnnnnneessss's?"* and once again, they've actually heard you say the word 'idiot' to them.

Again, they may well have told you all the bad stuff and drawbacks of their job if you hadn't, in their mind, demeaned their situation and told them they're stupid, but now they're more likely to be on guard against any co-operative interaction with you about the business opportunity. Prospect lost.

My preferred way to respond to such responses would be: *"The supermarket do some terrific own-brand stuff don't they?"* or *"Super Power – great, they're pretty good aren't they?"* or *"Jones's Coffee Shop – excellent – do you enjoy it?"*

Because I haven't insulted their choice, they're more likely to share with me their true feelings and since most people like to share negatives rather than positives, there's a good chance they'll start telling me what they feel about the Super Power customer service experience or how the supplements from the local supermarket are cheap and not really working, or how they feel they have hit a brick wall in their career and they're working too many hours.

So next time you're about to respond to a prospect when they're telling you of a decision they made, be careful not to call them a silent 'idiot' ...

 Leaders' Tip If your team member is not getting many sign-ups or appointments based on their effort, you may well need to listen to some of their presentations or prospecting to check that they're not unwittingly saying silent 'idiot' to their prospects!

Tip 25 Building empathy

One tip that can certainly help you when dealing with prospects and team members, is the 'Feel, Felt, Found' principle.

When a potential customer or distributor, or an existing team member looking for support and guidance, tells you of an issue or an objection, rather than talk over them and tell them not to be so silly, the 'Feel, Felt, Found' method is a helpful way to continue the conversation.

For example, a prospective distributor says they don't think they'll have the time to fit the business in. Rather than go head-to-head with them arguing about whether they have time or not, it is more helpful to ensure they know you are on the same page. So, you could reply, *"That's understandable – I know how that feels as I felt exactly the same way when I first heard about the opportunity, but having got started, I have found it actually fits in great around the kids and we can work together to make sure you have a clear activity plan and I will be on hand if you need me ..."*

The principle works in any situation that you face with someone who is potentially swaying away from the outcome you are looking to achieve. Don't obsess about those words rigidly, the point is you just need to let your prospect know you understand their position, you (or others you know) have been in that same place, but it is workable and you are there to support them.

That's a much more positive way to move a potential negative over to a positive without trampling all over the person you're talking to!

Leaders' Tip This is an important one for Leaders too. When you get a team member telling you of a challenge they are having, they are reaching out for support. Telling them to *"just get over it"*, or *"well I can do it so why can't you?"* is not going to work for most personality types. By meeting them 'where they are at' with empathy you can help bring them to where they need to be without facing a stand-off or alienating them.

Tip 26 Getting a 'yes' and then buying it back

Warning! You can get people chomping at the bit with excitement and ready to sign up, but then, fearing any possible silence or them saying 'no' (*which they were probably not going to do*) you blow it all by saying too much – by continuing on with details that are neither interesting nor relevant to a new prospect and in doing so you give them something to think about!

Moreover, you make them feel that if it's this difficult to get a 'yes', if they have to go into the level of detail you are sharing and the time spent, then the business is not for them.

In effect what you do is you sell the idea to them, then you buy it back.

If you haven't read or listened to *Questions are the Answers* by Allan Pease, I would do so as this will really help you understand how to ask the simple questions to get you where you need to be.

Spare them the detail and simply ask them: *"So, would you like to give it a go?"* or: *"Should we get you registered then?"* or: *"So, shall we get your products ordered then?"* or *"Which of our packages would suit you best?"* (obviously your close needs to fit your business) or something along these lines. If people have further questions, then they will ask, and you can answer and then ask them the closing question again. Then you'll get an answer!

What doesn't happen is you talk and talk and talk and then they say: *"Okay, okay, sign me up pleeeeeaasssee!"* – so learn when to keep quiet, stop buying back the positive decision and you'll build your business more quickly and less painfully.

Leaders' Tip Getting your team to stop 'selling' and keep quiet and to actually ask a closing question is something you need to focus your time on. Get this bit right and your new team members will fly! Underestimate its importance and you'll always be wondering why growth is slow.

Tip 27 The alternative close

I'm not a major fan of teaching lots of sales techniques to distributors (and turning them into something other than themselves) but a few simple ones to help boost the chances of an appointment can do no harm.

When you're trying to put an appointment time in the diary, I have always found it useful to offer some alternatives to make a decision easier.

For example, if you say: *"Can you meet next Tuesday?"* then someone can easily say: *"No"*! But you are less likely to hear that answer if you give them a choice, so: *"When is best, next Tuesday or Thursday?"*

Now they have a choice to make and you have increased the odds of their availability, while also making it more inferred that the meeting is going to go ahead. What you will also find is that if they can't do either time they will say: *"Mmm, can't do Tuesday as I have golf, Thursday we have Marian's birthday dinner, but I am around Friday ..."* – result!

From there, you can narrow it down further – *"Afternoon or evening?"*, *"Would you prefer 6 or 8pm?"* – and then you have given yourself a much greater chance of getting the appointment.

 Leaders' Tip Simple 'odds improving' tips like this are useful to be shared with your team to help them – ensure you share yours as well but don't try and turn them into super-slick salespeople as most folk feel they haven't got the 'gift of the gab' so we must not make them think they need it.

Tip 28 — Getting contact details from cold prospects

You chat to someone at a party, on a train, when they have delivered something to your front door or when you are simply out and about; you build rapport with them, you want to talk to them about your products, services or opportunity, or indeed you already have done during your brief chat.

Possibly, you give them some information, a card or a DVD and they seem positive and amiable. But time is running out, you're all set to go your separate ways and you really want to get their number, but don't want to ask for fear of sounding like you're chatting them up or coming on too strong!

How do you get their contact details, rejection free?

There's one main way I have always used – it has never failed me so I'll share it with you now for you to keep in your armoury!

I simply say to people: *"Have you got a card?"* and what always happens is, if they do have one, they're only too happy to show it off. If they don't, they tend to, almost slightly flustered or embarrassed, say: *"No, I haven't but let me write my number down for you."*

I use that question even if I think they probably aren't the type of person to have a card as either way gets the result.

In this new technological age, younger generations may also pull out their mobile and simply ask someone to pop their number in the phone, or ask them if they're on Facebook – and I do use these on occasion too, but my trusty old favourite is the business card question – and it's never let me down yet!

 Leaders' Tip These quick and simple top tips are great for sharing with your team on a phone call, at a team meeting or on a conference call. Easy for anyone to implement and great to help your team get more people into their pipeline. Don't bombard them but you are likely to have lots of these in your locker that you don't think anything of. Get them out!

Tip 29 | Chicken list

I suspect that throughout Tip 7 about building your list, there were a whole load of people that came to mind where you thought: *"I'm not telling him – he's far too important"* or: *"I'm scared to speak to her."*

Add those to your list anyway. Even if you put them on a separate list called your 'chicken list'.

There's two great reasons for this – firstly, you can ask one of your upline or a buddy to make the call to that person and say *"You don't know me but I'm a colleague of your friends Sheila and John. I'm expanding my business in the south east and I'm looking for entrepreneurial types who might be open to making extra money and John mentioned you. Do you like to keep your business options open?"*

This call is so much easier for them to make as they are not emotionally attached and do not know the person, so they won't have the same fear of contacting them.

Secondly, by having them on your list, as your confidence grows you may well feel that you are happy to contact them yourself.

Remember, as discussed in Section 1, if you edit your list, you edit your income!

 Leaders' Tip Can you help your team with 'chicken list' calls? It's a great habit to get into. Assign some time specifically to build a 'chicken list' with them as you will find that simply by having those names down increases the chances of them talking to a person they would otherwise never have dared to.

Tip 30 | Don't be emotionally attached

Of course your results are important to you – you **want** this to succeed. It will succeed with a rational approach, in which you are able to position yourself in such a way that a 'yes' doesn't send you into delirious celebratory mode and a 'no' doesn't send you to the edge of the nearest cliff!

From a posture point of view, emotionally detaching yourself from the outcome, you will make the journey more peaceful and less stressful.

You can either have your journey to the top look like this:

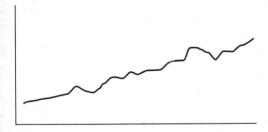

Or you can have a more stressful roller-coaster ride, like this:

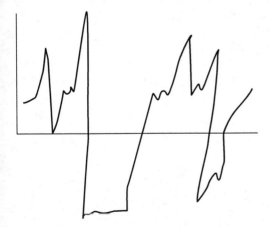

Ask yourself, which one seems more enjoyable?

It helps your posture as well and means that stress and emotion doesn't get transferred onto your prospect. I found life much easier for both myself and my prospects when I could say to them something along the lines of: *"There's no pressure either way – if you like it, great, if not, that's great too and at least we got to have a chat and a cuppa."*

The other key to not being emotionally attached is the realisation that you **are** going to succeed irrespective and so the answer from specific individuals has very little impact to the ultimate goal.

 Leaders' Tip Keep spirits high among your team members and ensure they know that **you've** had ups and downs too, and as long as they keep their focus, the ups will outweigh the downs.

Tip 31 Opportunity Presentation conduct

The Opportunity Presentations are fantastic for showing people the bigger picture and allowing them to see other folk just like them who are making a success of the business. This is fantastic for giving them social proof that the opportunity can work for them too (some companies will call these meeting 'Opportunity Presentations', 'Open Evenings', 'Business Opportunity Meetings', 'Career Opportunity Presentations', 'Business Evaluation Meetings' – whatever yours is called, just apply that title).

My advice is to try and get a seat near the front and although you may have heard the presentation before, pay attention, don't play with your mobile phone and do laugh in the right places! While the presentation is going on, do not whisper to your guest about what is coming next and, if they ask you a question, explain to them that you will answer it at the end.

After the event, do not redo the presentation. Simply ask your prospect: *"So, what did you like best?"* – once you have let them talk (and you have listened) and endorsed their thoughts it's time to ask them: *"So, shall we get you registered?"* – then be quiet and wait for their answer. If you don't have access to the internet and online sign-up facilities then you should ensure that you have a paper application form with you.

You should also keep your eyes peeled as to who is in the room that's in a similar profession to your guest or has a similar profile. For example, if your guest is a police officer, grab a distributor with the same background, or if they're a single mum, find the lady who did a testimonial to say she is a single mum. Let them circulate and mingle with other people similar to themselves and they will soon realise that the business can work for people like them.

If you ensure you put the dates of these events in your diary, for the local areas that are reachable for you, several months in advance, this will give you some target dates to aim for. Always try to invite twice as many people as you are hoping will turn up for these presentations, because some people will have to drop out due to family commitments, tiredness or general lethargy. If it so happened that you didn't have any drop-outs, you can simply ask other experienced distributors at the event to help you out.

However, it is good practice to have in mind the future dates, I would advise against keeping people waiting too long. They will go cold. If there isn't an event coming up near you, just get together with them and show them how the money works, or ask your sponsor or a local buddy to help.

These presentations will help you build your team – use them.

 **Leaders' Tip** Even though the opportunity presentations are not 'major' events, they are a fantastic way to keep your existing team motivated and associating with others. Ensure your team members know when these local events are and keep in touch with them to see how the invites are going. Gathering together in the bar area afterwards, even for a soda water or pot of tea, is where top tips are shared and belief is built. The strongest teams I notice, always have the strongest attendance at these type of events.

Tip 32	**Keeping prospects' details in your phone**

This is a simple but underused tip. Whenever I call a prospect from my mobile phone, or give them my mobile number, I always make sure I save their name in my contacts' directory on my phone, with their full name and a one-word clue about them and the words 'Biz prospect' or 'Cust prospect'.

Of course, it depends which handset you have as to how much of this is shown on the screen, but in theory, if someone calls you back or texts you, you can greet them instantly and warmly. It works a treat for building rapport and really helps people feel valued.

For example, your phone rings – you look at the screen and it says:

'Steve Hurst: Cruise biz prospect'

And you can answer: *"Hi Steve, great to hear from you, how was the rest of the cruise?"* even though you may have swapped details, given him your card and it was six months earlier on holiday, Steve is now feeling like a million dollars.

Or: 'Cheri Patterson: Cakes cust prospect'

So you answer *"Hi Cheri, good to hear from you, how are those lovely cakes you make?"* and again the rapport is instant and it avoids any of the: *"Who is this? Sorry, who?"* moments!

You'll find that you will chase more people than chase you, so at the very least ensure with those that **do** make contact, you give yourself the best chance of getting a great result.

 Leaders' Tip Good practice and useful tips like this need to be shared. Do it yourself and share it with your team.

☑ **Section 1: Getting Started**

☑ **Section 2: Skills**

☑ **Section 3: Good Practice**

☐ **Section 4: Building Trust**

☐ **Section 5: The Big Picture**

www.weslinden.com/79tips

Tip 33	**Don't take it personally – 'No' is 'No for Now' not 'No Forever'**

It is a widely-accepted marketing principle that people have to see something seven times before they seriously get into buyers' mode. So why do we think that it's personal when people don't respond the way we want them to, first or even second time with our network marketing business?

Make your customer-gathering and team-building a pipeline process rather than a 'hit and hope'. It's not **you** they are rejecting; it's just you may not have said the right thing, at the right time, for them to say 'yes'! There may also be some underlying issues they don't wish to disclose to you.

Change is something a large percentage of people are uncomfortable with; so asking them to completely change the 'norm' of buying into the supermarket-branded vitamins, or face creams, or spending their money with the conventional retailers for whatever your particular field may be (which we know will normally be too expensive for an inferior product or service provided by a faceless entity) – even if it's a change from negative to positive, it's still not something that everyone is immediately ready to do.

It means people need to think differently about their routines and making changes to what they have done before and consider if there's going to be any upheaval (which we know there won't be generally, but nevertheless we need them to come to that way of thinking without bullying them!).

Likewise, change from the mindset of swapping time for money, being an employee between 9 to 5 for forty-five years and then retiring on a paltry pension, to thinking as an entrepreneur and understanding the concept of working now and getting paid forever, while setting goals for luxuries and free time in the future, is a change. Again, negative to positive, but nevertheless change can make people a little uncomfortable and is something that people most certainly need to get their head around.

Consider that the first time they hear of your business, it is 'completely new' to them; second time it's still 'a pretty new concept' ... by the time it's cropped up between you for the fourth or fifth time, it is suddenly something they are more familiar with. Maybe they've seen mention of it in the press, or noticed a company-branded car or window advert, and the fact that you have lasted the test of time, becomes social proof that it works.

So understand that a 'no', is simply a 'No for Now' or indeed, 'Yes for Later'. In the book *Beach Money*, by Jordan Adler (which I would highly recommend!) he is very clear on the fact that his business was grown on the premise that most people say no, and if he likes them enough, he remains friends with them, keeps in touch with them, keeps them updated on the business, and when the time is right, they join.

Why does the 'no' offend us? Again, early on we are anxious for results and keen to make it work. Have faith that it **will** work, if **you** continue to! But it doesn't happen overnight.

I have introduced distributors fourteen days, fourteen weeks, fourteen months and indeed fourteen years after I first spoke to them about the opportunity. When people say *"no"* or *"it's not the right time"*, or anything that isn't *"yes"*, I simply say: *"That's no problem – I appreciate you taking the time to take a look – would it be okay if I keep you informed with how it's going from time to time?"*. I have never yet had someone say 'no' to that request!

Focus on the long term and you'll always win!

 Leaders' Tip Ensure your new team members don't fixate on the inevitable 'no' responses they'll get and make sure early on they understand the importance of keeping their 'No for Now' list while concentrating on prospecting for the people that will say 'yes'.

Tip 34   Be a product of the product

Ever heard of the successful car salesman who works for BMW but drives a Mercedes? No? I didn't think so, neither have I.

You cannot possibly hope to recommend the products or services of your network marketing company convincingly unless you are using them yourself. Of course, if it is logistically impossible for you to use one of your company's offerings, that is fair enough. But not using all the products and services for any other reason, is a costly decision.

Nobody will take you seriously if you are recommending something you aren't using and can't demonstrate without your own testimonial. Your lack of credibility will shine through and people will be less likely to sign up with you.

Even if they do choose to become your customer, they're less likely to take the products or services that you don't yourself use. So if the idea was for you to save money, you actually cost yourself money.

In the long term, the few quid each month you *think* you are saving will be cancelled out many times over by the monthly commissions and retail profits you are not receiving from the customers who don't take those products or services and from the distributors in your team who follow your lead and therefore don't convincingly promote too. Where your team can see you as a non-believer in certain areas, this filters through to them also and the compound effect of that is drastic.

Being a product of the product is the way to maximise your income and team growth if you are a long-term thinker.

 Leaders' Tip One of the first things you should do as a Leader is ensure your new team members are signed up themselves to be a consumer. They need to understand that this is a serious error in judgement if they don't and that, in theory, you really can't give them as much time as you would have done as they are showing themselves to be half-hearted.

Tip 35   Go on appointments with your team

The success of your team and growth of your group income is based partly on the help they get in their early days to get started. If you can help enough people get what **they** want, you'll get what **you** want.

Long gone are the days when people in this profession introduce folk and then sat and hoped – far better to get involved and help them get moving. Otherwise we just let people down, lose our own integrity and basically waste our time introducing them to start with.

Your aim is to have lots of people who are as effective as you, out and about building the business while you are working, eating, enjoying yourself and sleeping! The best way to ensure this happens, is to spend time with your new team members early on, and where feasible going on their first appointments to ensure they are confident and assisted with their early presentations.

As a new distributor yourself, be sure to ask your sponsor or someone in your upline team for this level of support even if culturally, this is not quite how currently Leaders within your particular business work.

 Leaders' Tip This will separate the players from the pretenders. If you're thinking *"what if I train them and they leave?"* I would ask – *"what if you don't train them and they stay?"*

Tip 36 Events, events, events

I've heard top Leaders say that attending a major event will *"put you six months ahead of the rest of the pack"*. I think this is incorrect; it could put your business five years ahead or more!

Think about it this way – the major events, as well as the smaller regional ones, will be packed with top tips, ideas, motivation, announcements and they tend to be pretty good fun too! If you want a small hobby income, then you'll probably get by without events; but if you want to build a lifestyle-changing income then you need to be at as many events as possible. Missing the major events because of a BBQ or a birthday party may seem like a good reason at the time, but I'd say that you are postponing your retirement party by several months for each one you miss. Unfortunately, I can see that with hindsight, whereas newer people cannot always share that perspective. So I need to ask you to trust me on this one – put the major Company events in your diary and don't let anything dislodge them.

I always used to think that when I have all the free time in the world, I can more than make it up to anyone who might have wondered why I didn't make their BBQ and that has certainly worked out!

It's just that **one** idea, mindset shift, top tip or way of saying something that could completely turn your success rate upside down and you simply can't replace that.

Leaders' Tip Play your part in ensuring that new people understand the importance of events, how great they are and how they have helped your business. Help them with diarising the dates so that nothing gets in the way and, where necessary, arrange car shares and even team socials around them.

There may also come a time when you have a desire for further learning and experiences beyond the Company events you attend. This is perfectly natural and I found this to be a great benefit to my business when the time was right.

Events such as the MLM Cruise (read Richard Fenton's & Andrea Waltz's book *Million Dollar Year*, which gives you a flavour of how powerful a learning opportunity the cruise is) and the Mastermind Event® are generic conferences where there's strict 'no sponsoring' rules and so you are entirely safe there with your team but you get to mix and mingle with some of the leading global network marketing professionals and hear keynote speeches from those at the very top of their game, while sharing experiences and good practice (and making friends) with people from all over the world, where you suddenly realise other network-marketers are your colleagues, not your competition (nor are they targets for your opportunity).

Tip 37   Learn to promote events

As valuable as events are for you, it is just as important (if not more so) to ensure your team attend them too.

Think about this – your team will be used to you and your take on things and they will be comfortable with what you have to say; but they need to be exposed to the bigger picture. They need to see hundreds and thousands of distributors all giving up a day of their life to realise they are part of something really big (much bigger than the local training venue and the coffee shop on the high street or the living room where local teams may meet); they need to hear announcements and get motivation from the Company Directors and top Leaders; they need to pick up golden nuggets of advice, great ideas and new ways of thinking from the 'movers and shakers' in the business; and they need to hear inspiring stories from people of all levels to help them focus on their own future.

Very often in my network marketing career (I have been a distributor with only one company but have spoken internationally for others), I will bump into people at events who say that their business turned around when they went to a major seminar and there is always a huge variance on which speaker or slot inspired them – this is the value of getting all of your team to all events – you just don't know what will inspire them, but you can be pretty sure something will.

Don't let technology get in the way of your promotion of events – do not just rely on text or email – get your hands dirty, get on the phone and speak to people, or talk to them face to face, and ensure that they have booked their ticket. Then follow up to double-check that they actually **have** booked it!

Many teams run social nights the evening before in local hotels or restaurants; or arrange shared transport to ensure they all arrive together.

One final tip – once you get your team to events (any event), ensure that they are not spending the breaks and the pre/post conference with the same people they travelled with. They can talk to them on the way back! Get them mixing and mingling with other people in the team they may not know, as well as others from different teams, while also introducing themselves to the Leaders and the speakers.

 Leaders' Tip Master the skill of promoting events and you're pretty much set for life!

Tip 38 Market your brand ... you!

When you go to the training sessions, the opportunity presentations and the bigger events, as well as social gatherings, you will get to see the better-known Leaders and those who you see on the Company videos as well as the top earners. Be sure to pick their brains and get a photo with them too.

In the days before camera-phones and Facebook, sage networkers would take a picture with the big players and put them in a photo album so they could show cynical prospects that these people 'really do exist' and show excited prospects that their new sponsor was 'in with the right people' to boost their credibility.

The same concept applies today, but with Facebook and Twitter and camera-phones, it is much simpler process and they can even just be stored in a special folder on their phone and use on their social media.

Another tip that has always worked well for me is with regards to collecting testimonials. You'll soon start to have happy customers – why not ask them to send you an email or write you a letter, explaining why they're happy and how you and your product has helped them? Keep them in a folder that you take to your appointments with you, so you can share some third-party experiences with your prospects while at the same time showing them that you are serious.

So, practise that smile and snap away – and start your testimonials folder now!

 **Leaders' Tip** Facilitate this process at gatherings by grabbing the 'faces' and getting them into a photo with your new folk. Once they've had a bit of encouragement from you to do this, they'll be doing it themselves in no time!

By having your own folder full of testimonials that you can show your team members, this will set the perfect example for them to duplicate.

Tip 39 Home meetings

When I started as a distributor my sponsors were very proactive in terms of running home meetings, either at their own house or in a local pub. It meant I had a regular meeting to go to, to recharge, to re-motivate myself, to pick up hints, tips and encouragement.

Sometimes these meetings were aimed at existing distributors, other times we would do little opportunity presentations for prospective distributors. They were invaluable for building a team.

Then, people like me got more heavily involved in the Company and helped them set up a generic, corporately-funded programme of events throughout the country, which meant there were training sessions and opportunity presentations scattered all over the place. This took the pressure off Leaders to run their own home meetings as everything was provided by the Company. It is great to have, but we became spoilt!

Over the more recent years, many Leaders have seen that they need the corporate system to get everyone started to bring them up to the same standard and for their ongoing development, but there is great value in having more localised home gatherings where people can really get to interact on a personal level.

Even if it just starts with you and a colleague in the local coffee shop having a regular half-hour chat, start with that; people can then join you as they join the team and it can grow from there.

The sense of belonging, identity, camaraderie and the ability to share ideas, tips and motivation on a personal level, is invaluable, and whether you have come from a team who runs these meetings or not, I encourage you to take the baton and ensure your emerging team have this base to keep them focused.

 Leaders' Tip Take note, give people something they feel part of and you significantly reduce the chances of losing them.

Tip 40 | Deadlines – avoid panic

Right from the off there are likely to be early bonuses and promotions aimed at rewarding your activity. Many of them are achievable without breaking huge sweat, whereas other promotions, while 'doable', will require some diligent attention.

Be sure you don't leave it too late – the anxiety that can come from needing a certain number of customers, volume or distributors to reach a target with a barely sufficient amount of time remaining, will so often lead to disappointment.

Try to get the targets 'in the bag' early on and then you can enjoy the journey in a much more relaxed manner!

 Leaders' Tip Help focus your newbies on getting targets met early, without pressurising them – and by leading from the front with your own targets you can ensure that this process is something they want to emulate!

Tip 41 Touch your business every day

We're all busy – that is beyond doubt. In fact, it may be true to say that most of us don't actually have any spare time when we join our network marketing business, so we have to **make** time for our activity and ensure we keep our eyes peeled when we are going about our normal, everyday activities.

One phrase that has stuck with me in my network marketing business and it has always served me well, is that whatever you are doing, however busy you may be, touch your business every day. Whether it's a welcome call, a follow-up call, giving a card to the lady in the local grocery store or a DVD to the postman, whatever it is, at the very least, touch your business every day.

Adopt this approach and your pipeline will always be active and you'll not struggle to find people to sit down and talk to about the services and the opportunity.

 Leaders' Tip New people may occasionally feel overwhelmed with what they need to do and have to learn. This is natural and we all tend to feel like this. Always remind them that just to touch their business each day will keep them ticking along towards their prize goal no matter how busy or flustered they may feel.

Tip 42 | Activity not results

I am not a big fan of distributors shouting about how many sign-ups they have had that day or month. I think this provides a deceiving statistic. You'll not find anyone who has a 100% strike rate and what I think matters more in this type of long-term business, is the effort you put in along the way. It's the activity that leads to results.

What distributors need to understand is, that if you focus on results only, you'll burn out very quickly due to the disappointments that will come your way whenever anyone says 'no'.

However, focusing yourself on the activity and judging your success by the processes, conversations and work that leads to the results (either immediate or sowing future seeds) rather than the outcome, will help keep your motivation high.

 Leaders' Tip When you start to build a team, be sure not to intimidate people by only reporting your success stories. Let the team know your results only come through your activity – and be humble enough to admit that you have your disappointments too!

Tip 43 Ask for help

There will be many people in your network marketing business who have trodden the path that you are now treading, at whatever stage you are on your journey. There is no monopoly on good ideas, so be sure to use those around you to help you in your journey.

Whether it be your sponsor, someone further upline to you, a local buddy, a Trainer, the support teams at Head Office, the senior Leaders, someone you meet at the local or national event, or even a colleague you get chatting to on the online help forum, if you need to chew over an idea, dissect why something isn't working the way you want it to, or get some fresh input, simply ask the question.

I think you'll struggle to find a profession that has such an open-arms approach to helping others, in many cases without financial gain – doubtless you'll then adopt the same approach as well – so use it to the advantage of you and your team.

 Leaders' Tip As a Leader consider you may not always be the person best-placed to advise a team member on a method or a query they have, so facilitate putting them in touch with colleagues and peers with other strengths who may be able to help and inspire them in different areas to yourself.

Tip 44   Don't underestimate coffee and wine

If this really is a relationship business, then social time is important too.

Some of the strongest businesses I have seen in this profession revolve around teams where there is a strong sense of fun and camaraderie that extends beyond the meeting room or studying scripts or business structures.

Team meals, bowling nights, group event-days (i.e. bike rides, abseiling, clay-pigeon shooting, BBQs and charity efforts) coffee get-togethers or a good old-fashioned chat over a bottle of wine or beer is a really important part of building the business. When people feel part of something and have a sense of belonging, they are more likely to see it through even when the going gets tough, because they know they have friends who are also colleagues who will be there to support them.

Leaders' Tip As a Leader you need to look to facilitate and organise this type of culture. You cannot look to such things as: *"How many customers joined my group as a result of having that coffee with Suzie last week"* or: *"It's three days since that BBQ and that damn Craig ate four of my burgers but hasn't got promoted yet!"*

You will not really be able to directly measure the actual result of such activities but trust that over time, this is a sound way to build your team. New people will come along and think: *"Wow, these people actually get on with those they work with – and they're nice to me too, I wanna be part of this!"* You can't put a price on that. If these events aren't happening in your area or aren't available for your team from those upline to you, then **you** organise them – after all, it's your name on the commission cheque!

Tip 45 — Daily contact with sponsor – don't be a lone wolf

When I started in my network marketing business, I spoke to my sponsor on a near-daily basis and other Leaders in my upline team with similar regularity. Whether it was for advice, information or just to check in and update them on my activity and get feedback on anything I could do better. That regular interaction, encouragement and a pat on the back kept me going as I always knew there was some positive input available.

While you relate to some people better than others, I naturally gravitated towards some people in my upline team more than others as I developed in the business and this daily contact continued as I was becoming a Leader in my own right.

I would advise you do the same as you start your business and thereafter when you're growing your own team – we all need a pick-me-up from time to time and some input from a different voice to help us recharge our batteries. Chances are that someone in our upline will have experienced what we are going through no matter what stage we are in our development and to be able to discuss those small matters is invaluable.

If you don't have someone you feel you can relate to in that way in your upline, then use the Company events and online forums to spot someone who you think you can interact with and ask them if you can have that line of communication with them – in all my time in the profession I would suggest you won't find many people who would say 'no' to this request.

Finally, don't be embarrassed – this is your upline's business too and they want you to develop and grow. Even if you feel you haven't got anything to say or things aren't moving at the pace you had hoped for, they will want to be in contact with you to help you manoeuvre around any pitfalls or issues you are facing and to flourish – so do get in touch with them.

 Leaders' Tip If you don't keep in regular contact with people – irrespective of whether they are struggling, a bit quiet and inactive, or whether they're a likely superstar, there's every chance they will fade out of your business.

Tip 46 — Don't tell everyone about selling products and services

It's unlikely that most peoples' lifelong desires will include selling lipstick, health shakes, bathroom cleaner or telephone services! It is not aspirational in the slightest. Therefore, when talking to someone about the business, do not let it revolve around calories, preservatives, calling tariffs or shiny surfaces.

When you are telling someone about the business, they are thinking: *"What's in it for me?"*

Not only that, but they are wondering: *"Is it simple? Could I do this?"*

If you have simply overloaded them with information about the products or services, or the prices and comparisons with the rest of the marketplace, you have subconsciously told them they need to be an expert on the particular industry that your network marketing business operates within, plus they now think they need to know the answers to lots of pretty boring questions they have never had an interest in before, in order to succeed.

Also, the more time you spend talking about detail, the less time you are spending talking about their favourite subject – **themselves!** Their goals, their aspirations and how an extra income would make a difference to their life and how you're going to help them achieve it.

Keep your enthusiasm for the products and services – naturally. However, keep it in check and ensure your prospect's priorities are the main focus.

 Leaders' Tip Keep an eye out for the enthusiastic team member who *luvvvvvvvvs* everything about the Company and check with them how their opportunity presentations are going, and role-play with them to be sure that it is not an evangelical product-fest with no attention paid to the prospect and their desires.

Tip 47 — Sell the presentation, not the products and Company

When prospecting people about the products, services or the opportunity, it is very easy to lose their interest by focusing too much on certain features, when in truth, you don't necessarily know exactly what their hot buttons are.

For this reason, focus on selling them on the idea of meeting with you for the appointment and presentation, rather than on the particulars of what you are going to cover. In some parts of the world, this is called *"selling the sizzle, not the steak"*! This allows you time to prepare and when you are face to face you can be more in control of the presentation, rather than taking random pot-shots at what you think they may be interested in.

You'll find this approach will help your success ratios!

Leaders' Tip When speaking to your team members if you learn they are struggling to get appointments for presentations, you need to spend time with them observing their approach. You can be fairly sure that, if they're not getting appointments, it's either because they are saying too much in the lead-up or they aren't even trying, so some role-play and teamwork will help you to help them overcome these issues.

Tip 48 — Too much info to too few people – tell less to more!

Occasionally someone will tell me that they are disappointed with their results over the previous weeks or months. When I ask them to analyse what their activity has actually been and with whom, we suddenly begin to piece together the realisation that, actually, they may well have spent too long chasing, or speaking to, not enough people.

So, for example, the time they have put into their business has been following up, speaking to and sending more information to the same prospect or prospects.

It is, of course, an important part of getting positive results that people are kept in touch with and followed up (and following-up precisely when you say you will is vital if you want people to take your business seriously) – however, the net needs to be wider so that you are exposing yourself to more people and, where possible, you are giving slightly less info than regurgitating the complete business manual front-to-back.

This is not advocating the scatter-gun approach, but it is important you are keeping the pipeline flowing!

 Leaders' Tip Do ask team members to show you their list from time to time – if they're obsessing with the same person and saying too much to them, it'll be fairly obvious when they admit how few of the people on the list they have actually contacted.

Tip 49 Read the news!

News headlines from the papers and the internet really can be your best friend:

"Redundancy in over-40s at all-time high"
"Obesity levels rocket"
"The Great Big Government Pension Rip Off"
"Energy prices set to rise"
"Retirement hopes dashed for millions"
"Government drive to make over-40s healthier than ever before"

Even today I still make sure that, when I walk into the newsagent or supermarket, I scan the headlines. If I see any headlines relating to the industry within which my network marketing business operates (whether good or 'shock horror') or economic, pension or job issues being highlighted, I will buy the newspaper, read the article, cut out the headline and stick it into a folder.

Why do this, you may ask?

Firstly, it gives me an insight into what the man and woman on the street have been reading and are talking about, which helps me with conversation-starters, whereby I can allow someone to moan about their situation and how this news is going to affect them, which opens the door for me to offer them a solution.

Secondly, it means I have headlines I can point out (sparingly though) when I am talking to people about the opportunity, ensuring that their mindset is realistic regarding to the gravity of the financial climate, which can ensure their mind is open to supplementing their income.

So, use the news to your advantage as you build your business.

 **Leaders' Tip** You can help your team adopt this mindset by initially scanning and emailing headlines and articles to them and offering advice on how they can use this to their advantage. Warning – them sending the headlines *en masse* to all their contacts or posting them on Facebook with the words: *"you're all doomed"* or similar is likely to alienate people. Subtlety is the key – for example: *"Worrying headline this morning for those hoping to retire before 70"* is more likely to initiate open-minded conversation than being too confrontational.

Tip 50   Always leave 'them' with a prospecting tool

When someone has come along with you to an opportunity presentation or you have shown them how the money works in your business, or left them considering whether they wish to join, you should always give them a physical prospecting tool – a DVD, CD or opportunity pack (not a web-link in this instance unless a last resort – it is harder for someone to lose a DVD or pack than it is to lose a web address). This way they also have something to show their partner to get another opinion or just to look at again themselves. However, it shouldn't be loads of information – just one key tool should be enough and avoids overloading them.

Likewise, when they have come to a presentation of any sort and signed up there and then, you should also send them away with a DVD, even if they have already seen it. Yes, this applies to people who **have** signed up as well!

Why? Well, buyer's remorse can sometimes kick in and it serves as a useful way for them to remind themselves of the power of the opportunity.

Furthermore, when they get home and tell their husband or wife that they've just spent money on a business opportunity that is going to take up some of their spare time, they may not always get a positive response, least not when they try and explain it, without any training and based purely on one sighting of their own. Inevitably this can lead to people dropping out before they have even started.

However, if you give the new distributor a DVD (or other prospecting tool), and tell them to show this to their partner, the chances of the business being properly explained and the other person buying into the idea is greatly increased.

The tools are there to help you – it makes sense to use them!

 Leaders' Tip Lead by example with this – make sure you adopt this practice. Then, when new team members have presentations let them know that they need to have a DVD or prospecting tool with them to give to the person **irrespective** of whether they sign up or not.

Tip 51 Daily method of operation

One underused, but very valuable tool, that many companies have, is a Business Development Plan (if you don't, they are relatively simple to create – speak to someone in your upline team for help) to track your daily activities. Very few businesses in any sphere will flourish as quickly as they should if there isn't some decent planning put into consistent activities for growth. Your network marketing business is no different.

This simple plan allows you to set some activity targets for the week ahead which you can track as the week moves on. Some of the activities may not float your boat but those that you are happy with can have some target numbers put alongside them so that you give yourself a better chance of completing the activity that leads to the results.

If it helps you work better, then share your plans with someone in your upline team or a Success Buddy to help with accountability.

It's another free tool that is there for your benefit – why not try it?

 Leaders' Tip Helping your team members get used to mapping, tracking and celebrating their activity on their journey will build your business. When someone is off-track and not getting results, it's worth getting a handle on their actual activity. This will likely help both you, and, more importantly, them, to see where things aren't working.

Tip 52 Love the phone

So often the reason that people are not progressing at the pace they want to is because they are not seeing enough people. The reason they aren't seeing enough people is because they're not actually arranging to see them and the reason they're not doing that is because they're not picking up the phone enough.

Why don't people pick up the phone as much as they should? Sometimes there is an irrational fear. Remember, FEAR stands for **F**alse **E**vidence **A**ppearing **R**eal. The phone cannot actually hurt you! In all my years of doing this business, I cannot actually remember anyone even swearing at me, let alone hurting my feelings with the phone. So get over it – learn to love it! Maybe make calls in pairs, or set fifteen minutes aside each day, or reward yourself after every ten calls.

Another reason may be that you simply can't find time to pick up the phone and make calls. Busy with housework, driving to work, children, walking the dog – excuses are never difficult to find! Think about how you can turn unproductive time into productive time – for example, have a Bluetooth headset in the car and make calls to and from work, or use it when you're out with the dog; get a wireless headset for your home phone and make calls at the same time as ironing. Using your time more efficiently will be the difference between success and failure for many people.

 Leaders' Tip Lead from the front – if you're making calls when ironing, driving, walking the dog or whatever it may be, but you are clearly using your time wisely, let your team know this when you speak to them. Firstly, it is polite to let them know they may hear some background noise, but more importantly, it plants a seed that they could be doing the same during their unprofitable moments in the day.

Tip 53 Networking group hunter

One way in which some of those achieving growing customer bases and teams choose to do their business, is through networking groups. These are organised events where lots of small business owners get together and swap business, referrals and contacts. There are quite a few of these organisations around now – some better known than others, some more formal and structured than others. Many begin first thing in the morning – yes really early! You can be finished before the conventional working day starts.

One guy I know well in the network marketing profession, worked full-time in a department store but still managed to attend a networking group one morning a week and get onto his department store shop-floor by 9.30am. This has helped put him in the top 0.1% of achievers in his particular business.

However, there are many more groups emerging at lunchtimes, evenings, weekends or over coffee. There are those for different age groups and for ladies or mums only. Obviously, this varies from area to area.

Here's a home truth, to save you from some frustration: many of the people that attend these events have been doing so for a long time. They will have seen many people come and go. If you have even an inkling that you can just swoop in for a week or two, or a couple of months, pick them all off one by one as customers and distributors, and then leave, you're wrong! If they sniff that you are not playing the game fairly, you may as well pack up and go home.

As an aside, you do no favours to either your business or the network marketing profession if you attempt this type of 'hunter' behaviour – so ultimately everyone loses.

Yes, it is possible that your product or service will be useful to everyone, but the principle behind networking events is **giver's gain** so those that succeed in these environments tend to be the ones who give referrals to others and are committed to helping others before themselves. Adopt that approach and the rewards will follow many times over.

Leaders' Tip Networking events are a great way to meet good prospects with a 'get-up-and-go' mentality who are useful to building a business. Work these right and you'll flourish, but if your team think they're going to swoop in and succeed, it's your role to help them see the error of their ways.

Tip 54	Avoid frustration – it's not easy but it's worth it

Like everything in life, there will be days when you don't know why you bother. You feel like you're putting in the activity but you're not getting the results. It's normally just a few inches away from success that many people fail, but they don't stick around long enough to find out!

If you're not getting the results you want, that's okay, just take a breath, relax, stay rational and focus on the big picture. Have a chat with those in your upline team and seek advice from local buddies and online forums.

Frustration is inevitable – but it's how we deal with it that shapes us. Try and avoid over-irrational celebrations for successes and likewise steer clear of dramatic over-reactions if things go wrong.

If you don't ever suffer frustration, you'll never be able to lead a team, because you'll never have true empathy with them when they have their inevitable challenges. Frustration is good!

Jim Rohn speaks of how we can control our emotions and frustrations by slightly changing our language. I took his advice early on and would use words like *"interesting"* or *"fascinating"* in place of frustrated expletives. *"Isn't that interesting?"* or *"How fascinating"* not only bring a calmness to a situation but they also act as an anchor to remind me that life isn't that bad and to not overreact.

Anything worth having is worth the investment of time. Sometimes that time will feel unrewarded, but focus on the big prize. Success in this business, whatever that is for you, won't be easy. But it's definitely worth it!

 Leaders' Tip Keep your team members focused on the big picture – don't over-dramatise the niggles; don't pour fuel on the fire. Help people learn from their challenges and move on towards the major goal.

Tip 55 | Social media conduct

This is one point that is only going to grow and grow as the years pass. Social media could have a hugely beneficial effect for our profession. It could also be an absolute nightmare.

Remember, the word 'social' comes before 'media', so my belief is you should use Facebook, Twitter, and LinkedIn to be sociable and friendly with people. To be **interested** rather than interesting. I don't believe your friends or those new ones you make want you selling to them 24/7, reposting sales messages and website links over and over again.

If you want to gain attention and make social media more profitable in the long term, rather than trying to get married on the first date, stop shouting about the offers and opportunities on your social network pages.

Judge this wrong and you will become a laughing stock rather than a professional and an entrepreneur. For every customer or distributor you gain, you have doubtless disengaged and turned off fifty more who will prejudge what you are doing and take no further interest in what you have to say.

Why not take a different approach to your social media messages – for example:

"It's great to only be working four days a week now."

"Sports day was fun – Henry and Olivia did well – but why was I the only dad there?"

"Loving the clever, new gizmo which keeps food fresh for longer."

"My energy bill is here! It seems silly I get excited about it I know – but I do now!"

"Looking forward to our little break next weekend – three holidays in a year would have been impossible two years ago."

"Just enjoying a coffee and then off to the gym. Love the spare time my new business gives me."

"What a fantastic evening – I LOVE being around such positive people so different from the normal workplace."

"Bizarre to think I am 6 kg lighter now, in just four months."

"I see XYZ are putting up their prices again. I'm glad we don't need to worry about that anymore."

"Got told I looked 25 today. Not bad for a 42-year old! Loving my new skincare range."

"Jayne starts school tomorrow but I'm so glad I'm one of those mums who can work from home for myself now rather than go back to work ..."

Creating curiosity for those in your social circle rather than directly selling to them is far more likely to get people sending you a response or a direct message asking you what you are up to. Although this may not happen the first time they see your post, it will have a compound effect and over time people will notice a difference and comment.

You are advised to private message them in response rather than have an online conversation which others can see (for example, on your Facebook wall) as this prevents others interfering in your conversation or prejudging what you are going to say prior to you being able to interact with them directly.

Be more creative with your social media posts and you'll see the results over time – **and** keep your friends in the process!

 Leaders' Tip This is another point where you need to lead from the front – watch what you yourself are posting. Some of the rather more brusque Leaders (they'll be the red types if you understand *Colours* as discussed in Tip 5!) will say *"It's none of your business what other people think of you"*. Wrong. It most certainly is your business what people think of you **and** your venture, because if they don't like you or trust you, they won't be joining nor will they be referring anyone to you.

Keep an eye on what your team members are writing and if you need to speak to them about it, be sure to do so to avoid them blowing out their prospects.

☑ **Section 1: Getting Started**

☑ **Section 2: Skills**

☑ **Section 3: Good Practice**

☑ **Section 4: Building Trust**

☐ **Section 5: The Big Picture**

www.weslinden.com/79tips

Tip 56 | People can smell desperation

It is accepted that dogs can smell fear. In the same way, humans can sense desperation in other people.

I often have people tell me they are not getting the results they expect based on their efforts, whether it be no-one will agree to an appointment, no-one is signing up when in a presentation, or people aren't biting when prospecting them face to face.

They may well be saying the scripts word for word, and they could be giving the presentation perfectly, but very often there's a desperation that is present in the manner of the distributor, either because they are chasing a bonus or promotion, or because they are simply very keen to get their business off the ground.

However, this enthusiasm needs to be correctly harnessed because your prospects will sense if there's desperation in the air and there's nothing as likely to turn people off as this.

Relax, breathe, smile and know that the decision of this prospect does not make or break your business.

 Leaders' Tip Look out for this in your new people and be sure to alert them to the possibility that this is how they may be coming across, particularly if they are putting in a lot of activity with not enough results.

Tip 57 Make friends to make friends

One area where people often struggle to pitch themselves well, which often leads them to ask why no-one ever calls them back anymore and why their party invites have dried up, is because they subconsciously no longer see their friends as friends, but instead see them as targets.

This will cost you friends and it will actually cost you business. Your friends do not want to see you preying on them every time you speak or meet up.

Likewise, new friendships should be born naturally for the best and most wholesome intentions, and not because you smell a utility bill payer, or a person is eager to lose weight, look young or is expressing some discontent over their financial situation.

I am very much an advocate of approaching those who know, like and trust you, in the early stages of building the business, but this must not take over the friendship, irrespective of whether they say 'yes' or 'no' at first. It is only through you being a genuine friend that people will support you in business and will continue to support you in your life.

 Leaders' Tip Ensure your team has faith in the concept of the long-term friends we make before and during someone becoming part of your network marketing business. Relationships, trust and friendships are built for the best and most honest reasons. They need your help understanding that it's the relationship that is key and that the sign-up can come when the time is right, providing they like you enough.

Tip 58 | Listen more

Most people like the sound of their own voice – so let them talk! It's better to be interest**ed** rather than interest**ing**!

The temptation – particularly for less experienced distributors – is to do lots of talking and show your prospect how clever you are, whether it be about the customer proposition or the opportunity. The truth is, your prospect prefers the sound of their voice to yours!

By letting them talk you are able to hear their hot buttons, find out more about their goals and wishes, and it is a great way of building rapport and trust. People tend to do business with people they like, so listen more and speak less, and they'll love you!

 Leaders' Tip When a new team member isn't getting the results that their efforts suggest they should be getting, make sure you find a way to hear their presentation and some of their prospecting calls – whether it be in person, over the phone role-playing with you, or by getting them to record themselves on their smartphone and letting you listen. This coaching will be invaluable and will ensure they are doing more of the right things! A great tool to help you with this is *Questions are the Answers* by Allan Pease.

Tip 59 — Plan the free time you have for the business – but don't forget your family

One of the many reasons that people join this profession is to create a better lifestyle and generate more choices for themselves and their family.

In the short and medium term, this will mean some sacrifices. It may mean missing an occasional birthday or BBQ but this will be more than made up for by the choices and opportunities you will have in the future as a result of the occasional sacrifice.

However, while on your journey, do ensure that your diary includes some family and/or partner time. If you never make time to go to the cinema, or out for a drink, a day-trip or even just walk the dog together, you'll naturally lose support from those for whom you are working hard.

You need those close to you onside and invested in what you are aiming to achieve. Even if they are not active in the business, ensure they know of your successes and invite them to the occasional Company event and also social gatherings where they get to meet other people. Keeping them in the picture, engaged, and not neglecting them, will ensure they back you, making the whole journey much more pleasurable and tension-free!

 Leaders' Tip Lead from the front with this one – ensure your team see and know that you're making time for those close to you so they are totally clear that this is to be encouraged and that balance is important.

Tip 60 | Know when to move on

Ensuring that someone becomes a customer, a distributor, or even agrees to see you for an appointment is not a 'win at all costs' scenario.

I am absolutely all for the 'never give up' mentality, but there is a lot to be said for knowing when the time is right to give someone space, and respect that their head isn't in the right place to make the decision you are looking for.

Making sure you take this type of stance will both free up your time to speak to people who are ready to hear you, and retain your friendship and likeability with your prospect so much so that the next time, or the time after, they'll be ready to listen.

 Leaders' Tip Learn to spot when your new team members need to focus beyond the one prize prospect they have in their mind and guide them on this tactfully!

Tip 61 | Mass emails

We've all been there – you're really excited about your new business and you want to shout it from the rooftops, or there's a great new offer and you want to share it.

Mass emails are not the way to do it. People are savvy enough to tell when something is tailored personally to them or when they are on the receiving end of a sales message sent to lots of people. They withdraw when they realise this and you lose them for the future.

If mass emails were the way to build the Company who you represent, then why would your network marketing business need you to do it? They could simply get a computer system to do the work automatically and then pick up the rewards! What is unique about our profession is the personal touch which no corporate entity can ever do alone without **you**.

Keep communication personal, focus on the individual and in the long term you'll fly!

 Leaders' Tip When your newbie starts to ask you about what to write in emails to everyone they know, you need to step in. It's not a numbers game when it means alienating people from ever taking your new distributor's business really seriously.

Tip 62 | Speaking too loudly at a party

Parties are social occasions for you to mix and mingle with old friends and make new ones. Be cautious not to become typecast as a bore or a salesman by pitching everyone as soon as they arrive in your field of vision!

Speaking too loudly about what you can offer at parties is also likely to attract the loud-mouth expert who will think they are better educated at what you are talking about and will recite a horror story of theirs or someone they once knew who *"tried those pills"* or *"used to buy products from there"* or *"switched energy suppliers once"* or *"tried one of those home businesses fifteen years ago"*, which will be closely followed by some exaggerated precautionary tale of how the *"entire family was eaten by alligators soon after their house was repossessed"* – or something equally outlandish.

Not only does this moment cause friction and doubt with the onlookers, which you don't need, but it puts you into a conflict situation in a social setting where you are likely to find yourself feeling somewhat awkward.

Use parties for catching up with people and making new friends, but genuinely so – not just because they may be a prospect, which also allows you to sow seeds to make an approach in a more personal environment.

 Leaders' Tip Coach your team on the value of building relationships and sowing seeds, while learning when it is the right time to directly prospect. If this profession is about relationship marketing then the word relationship comes before marketing.

Tip 63 Personal contact versus text and email

The technological age has many benefits. To be able to send a quick text or email to someone, or chat to them via Facebook or Twitter, has helped us to keep in contact with more people than ever before.

However, language and intonations can be misconstrued through this method and there is no way for people to see eyeball-to-eyeball what your attitude or intentions are.

For years, businesses in our profession have been built through a cornerstone of personal relationships – either those in existence or those cultivated – technology can help, but not replace the hands-on approach.

The difference in how one feels when they get a handwritten 'Well Done' card, a personal phone call or a handshake is markedly different to how one feels on receiving a text or email, which, while thoughtful, is not as personal as genuine human contact.

In the same way, people will hear or understand the belief and enthusiasm you have when they can see it for themselves in your attitude, which is many times more attractive than receiving hyped-up sales messages via technological means.

Keep it real, keep it personal and keep it human and you'll not go far wrong with building your business.

 Leaders' Tip There is space for technology to be utilised for keeping in contact with your team, but ensure it is used in moderation and not to the detriment of a human relationship. Should you notice team members relying too greatly on technology, you need to have a coaching chat with them about getting the balance right.

Tip 64 | Looking for people who are looking

You wouldn't catch an estate agent trying to sell a house to someone who wants to buy a caravan and travel around the world.

So, never forget, we are looking for people who are looking. This means they are awake to opportunity and have an open mind. They may not *realise* they are looking right now, but when you start to talk to them, they are in a place where they are prepared to listen. This is all we can ask for.

People who are open to suggestion this year, may not have been last year, or may not be next year. So this is a great reason to keep in regular contact with people.

However, when you realise you are talking to someone who is currently not in the right place to consider a business opportunity or the services, that's the time to say to them: *"No problem – thanks anyway – do you mind if I keep you updated with how it's going for me?"* – nobody ever says 'no' to this and it means they become a 'No for Now' and allows you to speak to them in the future – and moreover, allows you to focus your time on looking for people who are looking.

 Leaders' Tip Like so many of the points covered in this book, your role is to help control your distributors' emotions when they get told 'no' and help focus their mindset on the long term, realising that this is simply part of the process.

Tip 65 | Irrational praise to team members

In those euphoric moments when a team member informs you that they have signed up a customer or a new distributor, we can sometimes heap praise on them that is not appropriate to the activity. Obviously, if you know someone has suffered a few knock-backs and really ventured outside their comfort zone, then they are worthy of a hefty pat on the back and encouragement, but be careful not to make them think they have 'made it' so that they put their feet up and retire!

Many people thrive on the praise they get and the recognition that is frequently bestowed in this profession, however, if you pitch the praise too high to start with, you may struggle as to where to go with that when they continue to progress! Imagine if you try and sing 'Staying Alive' by the Bee Gees, but you start the song on a note that is too high – you're going to be straining for those high notes as the song progresses!

Another point to consider as you build your team is that all of your distributors will work at a different pace. So three new customers or consumers in a week may be a walk in the park for one person whereas three in a month will be a struggle for someone else. When offering recognition at your events, team meetings or emails you should be mindful to recognise all those who are achieving a little less though still trying, no matter how their results may compare to others. There's nothing so galling to your team to consistently have one 'blue-eyed boy' heralded at every opportunity and not even a whisper about others who are also trying. Keep the balance and you'll be sure to create a culture where everyone feels appreciated and part of something.

 Leaders' Tip Recognition – it's said that babies cry for it, soldiers die for it – it's a really useful tool in your armoury, use it wisely and empathetically.

☑ Section 1: Getting Started

☑ Section 2: Skills

☑ Section 3: Good Practice

☑ Section 4: Building Trust

☑ **Section 5: The Big Picture**

www.weslinden.com/79tips

Tip 66 | Belief in yourself, your Company and the profession

There's no doubting that the profession works. It has been proven for many years now and has delivered on too many promises for its potential to be questioned. That doesn't mean that people who aren't in full possession of the facts won't occasionally challenge the sanity of your decision.

Likewise, the services and products provided by established and credible network marketing businesses have been proven to work and you can also believe in that. Many independent accolades, glowing satisfaction ratings and repeat customers would endorse your decision to have belief in the offering.

For over half a century, network marketing has provided incomes of all sizes to millions of people worldwide. Yes, there have been some more dubious businesses masquerading under the credible banner of our profession that have failed to deliver, but those are easily spotted when the cracks quickly appear. Clearly, our business has proven itself beyond any question.

So what else do you need to believe in? Believing in yourself is a key part of the success. You can believe in your business, the products, the services and the profession, but if you don't believe in yourself, people will smell it a mile off.

Uncertain, flaky approaches to people will not bring the result you are looking for. Nobody wants to be part of your experiment. So, if you feel you're a little nervous on the phone, or doing the customer presentation, or explaining how the money works, then spend time practising with your sponsor or a local buddy; role-play the simple words with a friend or partner and do it until you feel it just rolls off the tongue. If that means doing it for two hours a day for a week, then do so.

You wouldn't start driving without a few sessions practice with a mentor, so if you don't feel confident with your approaches and feel that your belief in yourself is lacking, then practise, practise, practise and you won't go far wrong. Thereafter, review and improve on your own or with a colleague.

The only caveat to this would be that you will never replace the experience you gain from real-life situations, but, if you're struggling with self-belief to begin with, then a little bit of practice can only serve to help.

Finally, remember, you can't win them all! Sometimes it just won't flow and your prospect will end up on your 'No for Now' list. But don't let excellence be the enemy of the good – you'll simply never get started if you wait to be excellent – only experience will take you to such dizzy heights!

 Leaders' Tip Your encouragement and belief in your new guys will make a real difference – ensure they know you are right behind them and that you know they can do whatever they put their mind to. Believing in themselves is a great reason why you must not do it for them, but simply help them to move their business forward, so that they start to foster self-belief and you don't create a culture of dependency.

Tip 67 More than just a hobby

There's a simple adage in network marketing, which is absolutely true in my experience: *"If you treat the business as a hobby, you'll earn a hobby income; if you treat it as a business, you'll earn a business income."*

This isn't to say you cannot make a success of the business in your spare time – you can. You can make a very decent income that will supplement your lifestyle. However, you'll never be Usain Bolt if you only go running once every six months; and you're unlikely to earn an eye-watering income by giving out one business card every other month and sending a couple of Facebook messages every quarter.

Be realistic – don't expect to match your day job salary in residual income based on minimal activity. However, find that spare evening each week and half-day at the weekend as well as taking the business (i.e. a business card; a DVD or a Company tool of some description) with you in your pocket (or handbag) and finding opportunities to tell people what you do in your daily activities, and you'll be surprised at how many people you have looking at your business.

 Leaders' Tip If you notice a new team member isn't really getting the results, there's a good chance they are suffering from 'NEPL rash' – Not Enough People Looking! A fatal illness that needs early treatment!

Tip 68 | Build your team earlier

Once you have done your initial training and are comfortable with the products and services (and have satisfied any other criteria in your specific business), you should look to start building your team. Having gone through the training or introduced some people to the products or services, you are perfectly poised to help someone else do the same and you have proven it can be done, so don't hold back from talking to people about the opportunity.

This also includes the very first people you speak to as customers. Your sponsor, or one of the Leaders in your upline team, can help you with speaking to those people about the opportunity if you need some support.

The sooner you start to build your team, the quicker you start to build your income, and more importantly, you'll have more people to work with and whom to start building a future partnership.

My experience is that the longer distributors leave it before starting to actively prospect people for the business opportunity, the less likely it is going to ever become a habit.

 Leaders' Tip Think 'big picture' – help your team get trained and get started but assist them to focus on the team-building aspect as well as building the customer base, rather than them just simply retailing the products and services.

Tip 69 When people say don't quit, you should listen!

Whether it be in conversation with members of your upline team, trainers, or talking to other distributors at Company events you will frequently hear the words *"don't quit"* offered to you as advice. Often you think to yourself: *"but I wasn't planning on it!"* – however it is very sound advice.

There will inevitably come a time when you think you aren't getting anywhere. Perhaps you feel you're not moving as fast as you had hoped, or you are disappointed by a no-show or a commission statement – this is part of the journey and every single top earner has experienced this – believe me, there will be times you feel like quitting or slowing down. This is an error in judgement – a surefire guarantee to failing to achieve the goals you joined for!

However irritating it may be when you are having a bad day, remember, this is a 2 to 5 to 10 year plan, it is **not** a 2 to 5 to 10 phone call plan!

One of my favourite quotes from Jordan Adler, in *Beach Money*, is: *"never quit on a bad day"*. Focus on the long-term goal and be sure to just keep going!

 Leaders' Tip A suggestion from a team member that they may slow down or quit is not a reason to disown them. This is where they need you most. Likewise, if someone stops returning your calls, they could be embarrassed about their lack of progress and may be feeling down about the business – it's here you earn your corn, don't count them out too soon.

Tip 70 — Remember the reason you said 'yes' to start with

There are very few people who go to the gym without a reason to do so. They will have a goal, a focus, a true reason and they will know that each time they exercise they will be bringing themselves closer to reaching that objective.

In the same way, there are plenty of people who have a gym membership, or lots of chat about the six-pack they're going to get, the weight they're going to lose or the marathon they're going to run – however, their true reason is obviously lost on them as they cannot get motivated enough to ever use the facilities for which they pay – we all know people like this. Indeed, gyms make more profit from the people who don't go (but pay), rather than those who visit regularly!

Why should success in this business be any different? Without a true, nailed-on reason to succeed, it is likely that your motivation could wane and attention wander to things that don't look so much like hard work.

Whatever your reason – and no reason is better than any other – be sure you really know it and indeed share it with those close to you where appropriate. Be absolutely sure in your mind as to what it is and ensure it is really clear, vivid and as detailed as possible.

For example, just saying *"new house"* is not enough in my view – same as *"new car"*, *"holiday home"*, *"kids" school fees'*, *"allow Dominique to quit job"*, *"meet new people"* or *"extra money"*. My belief is that to really have those goals as something you can believe in and aspire towards, to ensure they are very much real and alive, you need to be more specific and even state them in the future.

So for example: *"It is March 2018 and we have just moved into our new four-bedroom, detached home. The garden is around 100 feet long with a vegetable patch at the back, there is a double garage, a study and an open-plan kitchen. The house is a 1930s–built property that is along the King Charles Road."*

Or *"It's 25th December 2016 and we are sitting down to Christmas dinner with the family and Lyn is looking forward to sharing the news with everyone that she has been able to hand in her notice and will not be going back to work in January and will therefore be able to spend all her time with the children as they head towards primary school age."*

These are obviously examples and slightly dumbed-down from the detail you may wish to go into. However, you'll see the difference between a very clear vision and direction spoken with future certainty, versus a vague reference to what you might like. Network marketing professional Chris Williams released a very good CD set which makes helpful listening for people in our profession who are looking to set goals effectively, called *Don't Just Dream It … Do It – Goal-Setting that REALLY works for network marketers.*

Many years of spending time with those who are succeeding in building their business tells me that those who have very clearly defined goals tend to do much better than those who have vague, non-specific goals.

It may take a little time and it may seem a little challenging – you may even need some help from a mentor or sponsor to do this well, but it's very much worth clearly defining your reason for starting this business.

When someone told you about your network marketing business, you said 'yes' for a reason. Maybe it was for several reasons. All of them were very valid at the time and undoubtedly (based on the proven success already seen within the business), achievable.

A slow start or a couple of knock-backs do not make those reasons any less real. They may seem a little further away if time is a problem or if you haven't bothered to learn and practise the skills, and follow the system. However, that doesn't mean they are less achievable than they were, it just means that you may have to realign your plans, priorities and focus. It is vital to realise that you can achieve almost anything you want to from network marketing (but it doesn't happen overnight).

It's very, very rare to learn that someone has found a viable and realistic vehicle to help them achieve significant goals once they put their network marketing business to the side. That isn't to say people can't have creative ideas to build their financial freedom, however this is a tough economy, the world has changed a lot over the last few years and the chance to build a residual, walkaway income, is unique. I would go so far as to say we will **never** see these kinds of opportunity in any other profession.

Leaders' Tip Your team members need **your** help to create a clear vision for **their** future and identifying their true reason – be sure to provide that help. Then, you need to ensure your goals are big enough to encompass the goals your team has. I have often pinned key team members' goals up on my wall so I can remember what we are all working towards. Ensuring you know why your new team members joined to begin with will help you realign them if they go off-piste.

Tip 71 | Eat the elephant in small chunks

I am a big fan of goal-setting, stating intentions and making promises to yourself about how great the future is going to be. Very little significant happens when you don't set specific goals.

However, just saying it doesn't make it happen! It requires action also. Significantly though, it needs you to take some simple baby steps as you are getting started and moving your way through the plan to grow your business to wherever you need it to be in order to achieve your ultimate goals. It is important you focus on these as you begin your journey with, of course, an eye on the final destination. Not achieving a small goal is part of the journey from time to time and should never be a good enough reason to prevent you reaching your ultimate target.

Celebrating and recognising your small achievements and indeed rewarding yourself with something tangible as a 'pat on the back' for each marker you reach, is well worth doing. It could be a trip to a spa, a meal out, a bottle of wine, a new pair of shoes – but something cheerful that you can both look forward to, as well as to remember that achievement, makes the hard work worthwhile. If you only spend any bonuses you pick up, or indeed your monthly commissions, on council tax and petrol, it will probably make the journey to your ultimate goal less memorable and enjoyable.

 Leaders' Tip Be sure to celebrate team members' achievements with personal contact and a proper pat on the back and make sure you ask them what they are doing to celebrate to ensure that they are rewarding themselves properly.

Tip 72	**Find out who is successful and get close to them**

There's an easy way and a difficult way to succeed. Personally, I make no secret of the fact that I spend a lot of time finding out who is good and successful at what I want to be great at, and then following their lead.

That can simply be watching their Facebook, Twitter and blog updates or, if feasible, by getting close to them. This means introducing yourself at seminars and presentations. Depending on how they respond, I would try and get their contact details and again, where appropriate, either then or in the future, offer to buy them lunch or coffee, in order to pick their brain.

I think this is the easy way to succeed compared to the more complicated way of making lots of mistakes yourself. Indeed, this could speed up your success by months or even years if you are really diligent about studying those who have succeeded before you.

 Leaders' Tip Ensure you encourage your team members to mix and mingle at events very early on in their careers. Someone may say the exact same thing that you say, word for word, but it may strike a chord with them because of the different character.

Tip 73 Too much thinking and planning

There are some distributors who I speak to who have not progressed from one month to another, but they assure you that they are planning their big assault. Planning who to call, planning what to say and planning how to do the presentation.

Alternatively, they simply spend a lot of time thinking about the business, contemplating the benefits and the drawbacks, thinking about how perfect it would be if only this or that happened, thinking about how great it'll be when they are successful and thinking about what might happen if someone says something or nothing!

This is okay when lying in bed or in the bath, however it is not a substitute for activity. You do not get paid for planning or thinking so use your time wisely and make activity the priority.

 Leaders' Tip As a Leader you need your radar on when your team members are constantly telling you about their 'plans' but not actually acting on them. Spot the regular promises of greatness which fail to deliver a result and find tactful ways to discuss this with them – they may well be in need of some help or guidance.

Tip 74 | Meet me halfway

There's an old wives' tale of the chap (let's call him Jim) who is down on his luck and prays to God that he wins the lottery that weekend. Sunday comes and he didn't win. He looks up to the sky and asks God why he didn't make him win and solve all his problems. God looked back and said: *"Jim, I tried my best – but at least meet me halfway – buy a ticket."*

This concept of 'meet me halfway' is a fantastic one for a profession like ours, where people are only promoted based on reward for their own effort. Nobody falls on top of the mountain. In this profession it's the few who choose rather than the chosen few who flourish.

Hence 'meet me halfway' takes on greater meaning. It's true to say that most of the network marketing businesses I know of provide fantastic customer offerings, great training, terrific incentives and payment plans that work if you do. Our job is to meet them halfway and introduce new customers and team members to the business, creating volume and growth for the Company.

Your Leaders should provide practical experience, encouragement and moral support for you as you build your business, however, they can't do it **for** you – you need to meet them halfway and put in the activity which demonstrates commitment and will lead to results.

As you build your team, this principle continues. You can be there for your team members, helping them get started and motivating them to succeed, but ultimately they must also meet you halfway and not expect you to do it for them, but instead do it **with** them.

Master the 'meet me halfway' concept, both in your own activity and that of your team, and you'll have a business success that offers you some serious choices in the future.

 Leaders' Tip To quote the great Jim Rohn: *"You can help a thousand but you can't carry three on your back."* However much you think you're Superman – and even if you feel that doing everything for people is going to build your business – you're not, and it isn't! To coin another well-known phrase: *"Give a man a fish and you feed him for a day. Teach a man to fish and you feed him for a lifetime."*

Tip 75 | Don't let television steal your dreams

Don't panic! I am not about to say you should become a network marketing junkie and that you should shut yourself off from the rest of the world and live in a fluffy bubble.

However, we do need to be conscious of how we feed our minds. Many distributors who build big businesses simply find they don't have time to watch trash on television any more.

I am all for relaxing and indulging in a bit of escapism from time to time, however, filling too many hours a day with this stuff will seriously hold back your business growth.

One quote I loved, which I heard from a very successful distributor I know within the profession, who juggles building his business with being a busy headteacher, was: *"A television will cost you £500 to begin with, but then it'll cost you £25,000 over the next five years."* Think about that carefully and you'll understand why.

As time moves on and your positive mindset becomes one full of possibility, you may even find the news can become something you steer away from. Sensationalised stories about war, fights, poverty and conflict is not always the best recipe for keeping yourself upbeat!

I know one distributor who never really seemed to get off the starting blocks, who, when we had a proper chat one day to see what was going on with her business, admitted she listens to a radio station with rolling news and tends to have a dedicated news channel on the TV at home most of the time. I am not saying this contributed towards her lack of achievement in the business, however, would this type of brain fodder really be conducive for positive, focused action?

Everything in moderation, but be mindful with what you fill your mind.

Leaders' Tip As a Leader be careful not to spend too much of your time writing about your favourite reality TV programme on Facebook or talking about celebrity tittle-tattle too much during the lunch break at Company events. Why not? Your team will follow you – if you want a business that is full of people who spend their spare time watching an electronic income-reducer instead of building their dreams, then let them know you spend your time watching *X-Factor* and *Big Brother*. Instead, set an example that says you're building a better future and you give yourself half a chance!

Tip 76	Sulking costs you money!

Stuff happens. Such is life. Not everything is perfect.

I have seen many incidents where a distributor goes into a long sulk because they get hacked-off with something the Company may have made an error on, or a couple of rejections, or lack of motivation, frustration and anything else that people experience as they build their own business.

Sometimes this sulk leads to a period of inactivity; a self-enforced rest away from any business-building. I am all for taking a deep breath and a glass of wine to chill out, to clear one's mind. However, dipping out for three months, particularly if you have a team, will cost you far more than three months in the long term. Quite simply, if you're looking to build a true walkaway income, this won't happen by walking away too often, too early in your career.

When you decide to get back to business, guess what? Many times, I have seen it take people the same period of time to reconnect themselves into the business, if not twice as long.

Why would this be? Firstly, you need to familiarise yourself with the forms, brochures and website again and perhaps revisit the training. But secondly, and far more significantly, your pipeline has dried up. Yes, those people you needed to contact, follow-up, catch up with, chat to again, will require you to reopen the door with them but now they're cold, not warm! Plus, because you have been striking, you've not been talking to others and adding them to the pipeline, so you really need to work hard to get the wheels turning again. If you have a team and you go on strike, you can reasonably expect that it won't be functioning at full throttle when you return.

This leads me to conclude that it is much better to try and put any irritating issues into perspective and thus retain your momentum, rather than allow an issue to not just set you back the time for which the sulk lasts, but a much longer period of time when you decide to pick up your tools again!

Leaders' Tip If you want to avoid having to start new legs from scratch keep on top of this one, ensuring your team members have your support when they have an issue but that you do not over-dramatise it or get caught up in their story. Discuss it, offer advice, try to resolve it, but ensure they know they need to move on. Ensure that negatives only go upline and never downline or sideline. Only positives should ever travel down from you to the team. There can really be no issue that is so big that it costs time in the quest towards meeting their goals. The important thing to think of is, do they want to be right, or achieve their goals?

Tip 77 Bigdealitis

I regularly have distributors tell me about the next big customer or team member they are about to introduce and how, if they can just get this one, everything will change.

This is not true. While a big, high-spending customer is lovely and a new distributor whom you perceive has a massive database is great, it's important to keep your emotions in check and focus on getting the little things right too.

I have always been fascinated by the people who focus purely on the one big deal, thinking that if they just pull that off, they'll be able to retire. While these can be brilliant if they come off, you can easily lose focus on the day-to-day bits and pieces, then if it doesn't come off (which is what can happen in the real world) you have not progressed at all.

I always remember an example of when a distributor had actually signed up a supposedly 'big fish' distributor who had promised they were going to sign up thousands of new customers each month. This became all-consuming and quite a distraction. As it happened, they ran a business and one of their staff members decided to join as a distributor and a couple of years later they had hit their first two promotions, introduced a large number of customers and qualified for the Company car scheme, whereas the 'big fish' (with all their big promises) was no longer even registered as a distributor!

In the world of David and Goliath, the unlikely triumph actually came from another ordinary distributor, rather than the big deal.

This is not intended to distract you from opportunity, but to remember where the bread and butter is and anything beyond that is simply a bit of jam on top!

 Leaders' Tip Your team members will get distracted by this type of exciting deal or prospect from time to time. Help them and work with them on it, but ensure they are keeping the rest of their pipeline topped up and not neglecting the bread and butter.

Tip 78   Chasing several networks

There are lots of very good network marketing opportunities available, along with a few that masquerade as one but don't deliver on their promises. Network marketing has proven itself to be an extremely credible profession that delivers on it's promises.

I am a great believer that if you chase two rabbits you tend to get no dinner. Once people become aware that you have an interest in additional income, with your involvement in network marketing, you may occasionally get invites to consider other business opportunities.

You should be very cautious about becoming a 'big deal chaser', always hoping to find a get-rich option (which simply doesn't exist for anyone other than those who will run off with the profits eventually) and most certainly avoid being seen as a network-junkie who not only can *"provide you with essential oils for a healthier lifestyle whilst helping you with your utility bills but also with bin bags that last three times longer than normal, as well as skin cream to make you look younger and a miracle cure for your arthritis!"*

It simply doesn't come across as credible if you are offering your prospects fifteen different things at once and it most certainly does not show you to be someone to be followed, by others looking to make an income, who are looking for a clear direction, if you are juggling various opportunities and trying to show them how to do the same. Nobody wants to be part of your experiment.

If you are happy that your Company is the right vehicle for you, then keep focused, avoid distraction and you will win through.

Leaders' Tip The moment you pitch any of your team on any other opportunity than the one that you/they are involved with, you create a culture within your organisation that you'll not be able to change. You send out a message that says you're not wholly committed to making this business work and you lack belief in it. Likewise, if you spot any team members that have got distracted with other things whether it is through hearsay, or because they pitched you, you need to very quickly get on top of this and let them know the pitfalls of becoming a network-junkie.

Tip 79 Expecting to be 'rich' too soon

Here's another fact that catches many people out – so often people over-estimate what they are going to earn early on. They confuse 'thinking time' for actual activity and fail to remember that we are rewarded for results.

They compound this by failing to properly understand the payment plan which leaves them confused as to why they are not retired based on the spend of a handful of customers.

It is important for us to manage these expectations, and, where possible, see the early money earned as 'fun money' and not expect it to pay the mortgage after a few weeks.

If you can grasp the compound effect of your efforts over time in financial terms, you'll see that in many respects this could be seen as a business that underpays your actual time and effort in the early days, but grossly overpays your specific monthly input in the years that follow!

Sadly, some people aren't warned about this and can't get their head around it – they don't see it through so never get to understand the profound effect the business can have in the future. Please, please, don't be one of those people.

 Leaders' Tip It's always a good idea to ensure you have some team contact on or around commission day. Pick up those who are disappointed and build up those who are delighted. Good people will be lost if left to stew.

Lightning Source UK Ltd.
Milton Keynes UK
UKOW05f2243061213

222540UK00002B/2/P